The Nonviolent Revolution

**A Comprehensive Guide to Ahimsa –
the Philosophy and Practice
of Dynamic Harmlessness**

Nathaniel Altman

Gaupo Publishing
Brooklyn, New York
www.gaupo.net

i

GAUPO PUBLISHING

The Nonviolent Revolution: A Comprehensive Guide to Ahimsa – the Philosophy and Practice of Dynamic Harmlessness

This is a revised and updated edition of *The Nonviolent Revolution: A Comprehensive Guide to Ahimsa – the Philosophy of Dynamic Harmlessness*, originally published by Element Books in 1988.

Published in the United States of America by Gaupo Publishing.

ISBN 978-0-9979720-0-9

Dedicated to the memory of H. Jay Dinshah,

Founder of the American Vegan Society

and light bringer of ahimsa to North America.

Table of Contents

Preface to the Original Edition

The idea to write this book first came about in 1973 upon seeing a magnificent sunset during a journey to Bolivia. Though riding in a car with a group of friends, I seemed to experience one of those fleeting moments when one feels totally connected to life. I felt at one with the sun, the mountains, the clouds, and with the farmers walking their animals home from the fields.

Several years before, I had become acquainted with the teachings of Mahatma Gandhi, and was especially attracted to his views on *ahimsa*, the doctrine of dynamic harmlessness. As I viewed the sunset, I felt a strong desire to do my part in helping to save this world from destruction, whether from nuclear war or ecological ruin. For someone two years out of the university who loved to write, the idea of doing a book on nonviolence that would encompass politics, diet, economics, work, animal rights and human relationships was both exciting and appealing.

The original idea was to create an enormous work in several volumes that would include artwork, poetry, quotations, photographs and extended philosophical discussions about all aspects of nonviolence. It would be the most comprehensive and authoritative book ever written on the subject, and would be admired as a masterpiece.

However, after several months of research and writing, I realized that the book (or books) would not only be hard to write, but would be difficult to publish and even more difficult for most people to read. As I learned more about ahimsa, I saw how little of its essence I had integrated into my personal life. Although I took great care to present a "peaceful face" to the world, I often experienced strong feelings of anger, pride and jealousy. I also became aware of how my new intellectual knowledge made me feel superior to others, and how I would impose my beliefs in an aggressive, self-righteous and arrogant manner. At the same time, I judged myself severely for failing to live up to my nonviolent beliefs.

During this period, several close friends died through violent accident and suicide. As I had always believed that our friends reflect aspects of ourselves. I felt that these tragic deaths had some bearing on my own life and my unresolved issues regarding violence and cruelty. In addition to studying Theosophy, I decided to explore these issues through Core Energetics, a psychological and spiritual process which works - through special exercises - to release blocked energy and to discover the source of strength and wisdom within. For a person who related to the world primarily from a mental level, getting in touch with my body and emotions was important. I worked intensely with this process for five years.

Coming to terms with inner currents of violence and cruelty was both challenging and exciting. I began to be more aware of where I was not in truth, and how' this affected my relationships with others. I began to understand my defenses, how and why I would withhold my feelings, and how I would use spiritual ideals to mask arrogance and self-righteousness. At the beginning of this energetic process, I imagined that exploring and owning up to my cruelty and violence would destroy me. To my surprise, I found that by exposing and working with these aspects of my personality, I experienced a sense of relief, inner strength and self-acceptance. I began to feel more optimistic about my own life, and about my ability to transform negative currents of my personality into benign cycles of integration and well-being.

Despite this dynamic and exciting period of discovery, the perfectionist in me believed that since I was so far from attaining my ideal of ahimsa, I was not yet qualified to write about it. As there was no comprehensive book on ahimsa yet available, I was content to collect quotes of philosophers, writers, political activists, religious leaders and others which reflected different aspects of nonviolence over the past several thousand years of human history. In addition to selecting the quotes, I would write a short introduction to each chapter. This later became an anthology published in 1980 by Quest Books, a department of the Theosophical Publishing House, under the title *Ahimsa: Dynamic Compassion*.

For the next five years I busied myself with other writing projects, still feeling that because I had not reached the desired level of nonviolence in my personal life, I could not yet write a book on ahimsa that would more reflect my own ideas rather than those of others. In the meantime, I continued to amass a wide variety of books, journals, pamphlets and other materials relating to ahimsa for the book that would, hopefully, someday be written.

During a long drive through Western Canada in 1985, I turned off the radio and began to day-dream. I soon found myself think what philosophers would call "deep thoughts" and asked myself what I would do if I had one or two years to live. Pondering this question, the desire to complete "the ahimsa book"- even if imperfect - was the top priority. After I returned to New York, the sense of urgency to finish the book persisted. Despite my lingering belief that it may well take another fifty years to arrive at the level of harmlessness I hope to reach, a comprehensive and practical book about ahimsa was needed *now*.

The preparation of this volume has been a gift to me, and I hope it will be a source of inspiration, knowledge and usefulness to you, the reader.

Despite the challenge of living in a world that seems bent on violence and destruction, a live devoted to ahimsa offers hope for both the present and the future. To strive towards a life of dynamic harmlessness helps us to tap our deepest sources of compassion, truth and inspiration. It helps bring us closer to our innermost essence where love and compassion reside. By listening and responding to the often quiet voice of ahimsa within, we can begin to transform both ourselves and the world.

Nathaniel Altman
Brooklyn, New York
April 1988

Preface to the Second Edition.

Over the years I have written over twenty published books on natural healing, nature, metaphysics and relationship. Although I love these books as a father would love his children, I feel that *The Nonviolent Revolution* is the one closest to my heart.

The Nonviolent Revolution was published by Element Books, a progressive independent British publishing house, in 1988. Although the book was not a best seller, it received positive reviews in the press and eventually sold several thousand copies. It was also included on the recommended reading lists in peace studies courses at high schools and universities in the United States and Great Britain.

I had plans to revise and update this book sometime in the future, but the results of the 2016 presidential election in the United States inspired me to move this project to the front of the line. In addition to much-needed updates on facts and figures, I have been added new material that makes the book more timely, comprehensive and reader-friendly.

Many years ago I had the privilege of meeting Peace Pilgrim, an extraordinary woman who walked over 25,000 miles for over thirty years teaching about peace. At the time of our chance encounter at the Ojai, California post office in 1971, I was coordinator of publicity at the Krotona Institute School of Theosophy, and was able to help Peace Pilgrim make contacts with the media. I also attended several of her gatherings at local schools and churches. In addition to being inspired by Peace Pilgrim's powerful yet gentle personality, I was deeply moved by her simple, profound message of how inner peace creates the foundation for peace among individuals, communities and nations. She also taught how each one of us of can play a vital role in the global peace picture. Writing in her newsletter, *Peace Pilgrim's Progress*, she taught:

> We are all cells in the body of humanity - all of us, all over the world. Each one has a contribution to make, and will know from within what this contribution is, but no one can find inner peace except by working, not in a self-centered way, but for the whole human family.

Writing a new edition of this book has continued to inspire my own "journey towards ahimsa" that is still to be completed. Adopting a lifestyle that does the least amount of harm possible to other living beings, following a path of right livelihood, enlightened consuming, recycling, helping others, saving energy, and supporting individuals and organizations that work for good are essential for achieving both personal and planetary healing. Although born out of inner reflection, a life dedicated to ahimsa is both dynamic and expansive. It contains both the seeds of self-transformation and lays the groundwork for the transformation of society.

Nathaniel Altman
Brooklyn, New York
March 2017

Part I

Ahimsa Foundations

Chapter 1

Compassion: The Way of Planetary Healing

Ahiṃsā paramo dharma.
Ahimsa is the highest duty.

-Padma Purana I.31.27

FOR THOUSANDS OF YEARS, people the world over have sought to experience dynamic compassion (ahimsa) as an inherent, living, active expression of our innate goodness, of the God within. The term ahimsa (pronounced *əhim͵sä*) comes from the Sanskrit, and has long been defined in the East as "non-injury" or "non-killing". When viewed in a more dynamic Western context, it means "dynamic harmlessness" or more properly "dynamic compassion". This definition would not only encompass the renunciation of the will to kill or the intention to hurt any other living being through hostile thought, word or deed, but involves the conscious integration of compassion into every aspect of daily life.

Though the concept of ahimsa was spoken of in what is now India by Lord Mahavira (599-527 B.C.E.), Gautama Buddha (566-486 B.C.E.) and in China by Lao Tzu (sixth century B.C.E.), the doctrine of compassion was also taught by Jesus Christ and the Apostles. The essential doctrine of ahimsa has also been taught under a variety of labels by philosophers, political activists, scholars, scientists and religious leaders, including Henry David Thoreau, Sojourner Truth, Thomas Merton, M.K. Gandhi, Sir Bertrand Russell, Dorothy Day, Mother Theresa, Martin Luther King, Jr., The Dalai Lama, Robert Thurman, Peace Pilgrim and Rev. Matthew Fox.

It is also a major aspect of most indigenous cultures. For example, Native Americans, despite apparently having had little contact with the rest of the world, evolved a highly sophisticated planetary view based on the oneness of life and a deep respect for all members of the human family, including humans, other animals, plants, mountains and streams. Writing in *The Quest* magazine, Robert "Medicine Grizzlybear" Lake, a traditional Native American healer and ceremonial leader said, "Mother Earth is not only becoming polluted, but is also becoming weak and very sick... If she dies, we all die. It's as simple as that."

Lord Mahavira

Ahimsa: A Philosophy for the Strong

The term ahimsa gas long been misinterpreted in the West. Usually, the terms "passive resistance" and "nonviolence" have been seen as being equivalent to ahimsa, with "non-resistance to evil" following close behind. This has led many to view ahimsa as a wimpy, impotent way of dealing with violence in the world.

For many Westerners, ahimsa is an exotic term which brings to mind an image of a monk sitting on a Himalayan mountaintop- a quiet, isolated existence far removed from the challenges, conflicts and choices to be made in the day-to-day world. Others, who focus on its image of passivity, have viewed the practice of ahimsa as an avoidance of taking a stand in the face of danger of evil. Charges of "sitting by while your grandmother is being beaten" or "doing nothing while your country is being attacked by terrorists" are sometimes presented to illustrate this belief.

Ahimsa has also been criticized as being a dogmatic and absolutist doctrine, allowing little flexibility in its application. The image of permitting a swarm of locusts to lay waste to productive farmland out of compassion (for the locusts) is one example of this point of view; sparing the life of a terrorist who is plotting to murder dozens of people with a plastic explosive is another. Closely allied with this absolutist view is that the aspirant to a compassionate life is forced to adhere to a specific doctrine imposed by some outer authority- a situation that can only produce conformity, rigidity and fear.

On the other hand, some critics consider ahimsa to be a vague, sentimental and highly impractical philosophy, to be practiced by special people to a limited degree under ideal circumstances. The possibility that a "normal" human being living in Lower Manhattan, a refugee camp in Ramallah, or a suburb of Medellín, can practice ahimsa on a daily basis is regarded as a most unlikely and even absurd idea.

Dynamic and All-Encompassing

Actually, the true significance and scope of ahimsa is far removed from these perceptions. The teachings of dynamic compassion represent the essence of appreciation and reverence for life to be applied in every facet of daily existence, and represents a deep involvement in life and its challenges. Rather than merely a passive state of refraining from violence, ahimsa implies the active expression of compassion. It not only encompasses our philosophical attitudes towards war and peace, but directly impacts our daily interactions with our family, friends, colleagues and neighbors; the way we earn a living and how we spend our money; the kind of food we eat; our relationship with the environment; how we treat our companion animals; and how we view politics, business and education.

According to Gerald and Patricia Miche writing in *Toward a New World Order*, ahimsa is "an important concept not only in the development of a personal ecological ethic, but also as a philosophical foundation for the development of global structures that reinforce respect for, rather than violation of, the delicate balance and relatedness of all life forms". Far from advocating an escapist lifestyle, the true understanding of dynamic harmlessness encourages us to take personal responsibility to respect life and further it as much as possible. And to do so with joy in our hearts.

Ahimsa stresses positive action when one is confronted with evil or danger. It is not defeatist, it is not sentimental, nor does it imply an avoidance of discomfort, pain or even death. Ahimsa can be called the dynamic expression of compassion in some of the most dangerous or difficult situations.

Mahatma Gandhi, whose efforts to practice dynamic compassion led to his assassination in 1948, wrote: "Ahimsa is not the way of the timid or cowardly. It is the way of the brave ready to face death. He who perishes sword in hand is no doubt brave, but he who faces death without raising his little finger and without flinching is braver."

Ahimsa and Himsa

In order to better understand *ahimsa*, we need to have a clear understanding of its counterpart, *himsa*. In the ordinary sense, himsa is a synonym of the word violence- an overt act of destruction, the exertion of physical force which is meant to harm another, or a type of behavior designed to inflict personal injury to people or damage to property.

When this type of himsa is sanctioned by custom or tradition through the institutions of society (such as by government, business or schools) it becomes institutionalized. War between nations is the most dramatic form of institutionalized himsa, which can indeed be classified as institutionalized violence.

However, unlike violence, the word himsa can be applied to other harmful acts that do not involve physical assault: violent thought, hurtful speech, greed, deceit, and pride. In a broader sense, himsa can denote a *violation of personhood* when applied to humans, although it can be expanded to include all other life forms. When viewed in this context, any act of himsa- whether intentional or not- would violate the unique worth of each individual. And when considered in a deeper sense, any act which depersonalizes can be an act of himsa, because it transforms that person into a mere object to be used or manipulated.

Ahimsa forms the foundation of the belief system of the Jain religion, which is practiced by over three million people, mostly in India. Over the centuries, the Jains have enumerated no fewer than 432 types of himsa caused by thought, word and deed. Many types of himsa do not involve negative intent, and for this reason will not play a major role in our discussion here. "Necessary" himsa may take the form of a dentist pulling a tooth and causing temporary pain, or a surgeon cutting into a patient in order to save a life. Some forms of himsa are unavoidable. With every breath we take, we kill millions of tiny microbes. Insects and small mammals may be killed or injured in the harvesting of wheat. In addition to polluting the environment, when we drive a car there is the possibility of squashing a toad or other animal on the road, or killing some insects with the windshield or grille, even when traveling at slow speeds. Jain monks in India take their vows of compassion so seriously that they refuse to ride in motor vehicles, and are extremely careful of insects even when they walk along the street. According to the Jain text *Atma Tatva Vichar*:

> A monk has to be over scrupulous to avoid
> any injury to subtle or gross beings, while
> moving, talking, eating, drinking, rising,
> sitting or sleeping. This is the reason why the
> monks maintain a broomstick with them.
> With the help of extremely soft type of
> woolen threads of the broom, they gently
> remove any living insect which might crawl
> on the body, dress, or other utensils lest it
> might be injured.

Himsa: Four Basic Types

Although we'll discuss acts of himsa towards other kinds of beings later on, the first part of this book will deal with the more immediate aspects of himsa towards other people. These types of himsa fall into the following four categories.

1. *Personal overt physical assault:* This would include acts of violence like beating, rape, abortion and other personal attacks.

2. *Institutionalized overt physical assault:* Acts of terrorism, war, and police brutality are among the most obvious examples.

3. *Personal covert himsa:* This is the psychologically dangerous himsa where human dignity and personhood are denied. Examples may include hurting another person through thought, word, or deed; withholding concern and/or support when the situation demands it; and individual postures of racism, sexism and prejudice based on a person's religious belief, age or sexual orientation.

4. *Institutionalized covert himsa:* Where institutions like business, government, schools or religious organizations violate the personhood of society's members, whether by acts of commission or omission. Poor housing, racial discrimination, unemployment, disenfranchisement, and neglect of those in mental institutions and nursing homes fit into this category.

Covert himsa, whether on personal or institutional levels, is especially dangerous, because it is often subtle or otherwise kept from view by either the established media or the institutions themselves. As a result, it is often tolerated within the structure of society, where it is allowed to fester like an untreated wound.

Most of us, for example, are unaware of the homeless people living in their cars or on the streets in our local communities. We have no clear idea of how many people are in prison and how long they will remain there. We often have a vague idea of what actually takes place in a slaughterhouse or vivisection laboratory, even when located nearby. We often have no direct knowledge of what occurs when toxic waste from a factory pollutes a river because a group of business executives was uncaring towards the environment.

Often, covert himsa can go on for years before it becomes public knowledge. The sexual abuse of young people by priests in the Roman Catholic Church had often been tolerated (though even an open secret) until recently, when victims decided to pursue both criminal and civil actions against both the priests and the church hierarchy that protected them, as well as contact major media organizations, which began their own investigations.

We mentioned earlier that the word himsa has no exact counterpart in English, although the term "violence" is often used. However, when we speak of injustice, greed or racism, it is perhaps more appropriate to use the word himsa, or when applicable, words like evil, injury or harm. Hoarding the world's resources or having Mexican peasants grow strawberries for export instead of beans to feed their families may not be necessarily acts of violence, but well may be acts of himsa.

Advocates of ahimsa viewed it as the only alternative to himsa in the world, while maintaining that it would not necessarily be seen as a contrary force to himsa, because that would imply duality and struggle. Gandhi once compared the force of ahimsa to that of heat produced by the sun in its ability to melt snow and ice. He wrote, "The hardest metal yields to sufficient heat. Even so the hardest heart must melt before sufficiency of the heat of nonviolence. And there is no limit to the capacity of non-violence to generate heat."

On a practical level, dynamic compassion can be expressed in many ways, though they gravitate towards four major areas:

Non-Resistance to Evil (Satyagraha)

Rather than a passive term, the doctrine of "non-resistance" to evil involves combating an injustice with active love (known as *agape* in Greek). When applied to social problems or the world of politics, this aspect of ahimsa involves the practice of *satyagraha*, which means "soul force" or "truth force" in Sanskrit. Gandhi believed that the combination of truth (satya) and firmness (agraha) engenders– and therefore can serve as a synonym for– force. In practical terms, satyagraha would simply mean *holding fast to* or *adherence to* truth. Gandhi was probably the foremost exponent of satyagraha in the twentieth century, and sought to practice it faithfully in his campaign to secure the independence of India from Great Britain.

In many quarters, satyagraha has been confused with the philosophy of passive resistance, although there is a marked difference between them. Passive resistance, as commonly understood, implies the action of the weak, unarmed or helpless. It does not reject violence as a matter of principle, but because the means for violence are lacking. It can even serve as a preparatory stage for violence, or other acts of armed resistance. The underlying objective is to harass or manipulate the opponent into a desired course of action.

Satyagraha, on the other hand, rejects violence as a matter of principle. The idea is not to harass or destroy the opponent, but to convert or win him or her over by patience, honesty, sympathy or self-suffering. It is based on the belief in the inherent goodness of every human being, however deeply buried this goodness may be. "Hate the sin and not the sinner" was Gandhi's essential guideline for a practitioner of satyagraha, known as a *satyagrahi*.

While the work for an aspirant to satyagraha is primarily associated with political action, a satyagrahi can also devote his or her life to constructive activities in the spirit of service to one's community. Speaking out (and working) for animal rights, aiding the homeless, visiting the sick, writing letters to public officials, working towards sobriety on the highways, promoting good nutrition, and doing fund-raising for charities like People for the Ethical Treatment for Animals, Amnesty International or UNICEF are all worthwhile activities that promote peace and alleviate suffering in the local and planetary communities. Whether we support a campaign to end racism, promote adoption as an alternative to abortion, or plant trees in a poor neighborhood, we as individuals can do much to participate in the healing process of the planet on which we live.

However the most important role of a satyagrahi is speaking the truth. In a world where lying, deceit and manipulation are the norms– whether in business, politics or social interaction– the discernment of truth in daily life and its' active (though often quiet)expression, is considered the hallmark of an aspirant to a life of compassion.

Nonviolent Direct Personal Action

This more radical aspect of dynamic compassion can take the form of peaceful demonstrations, picketing, vigils, fasting, boycotts, raids (such as entering a laboratory and freeing animals that are being experimented upon by vivisectionists), blockades, publicly speaking out for truth and justice, and other active work for peace.

These activities can (and often do) involve personal danger, because we risk attack by those who disagree with us or who are entrusted with maintaining civic order, like the police or military. In some cases, we may need to protect another person who is being attacked, or risk personal safety by helping others during an earthquake, fire, flood or other disaster.

One case in point involved Gurudev Chitrabhanuji, a widely respected spiritual leader of the Jains. While walking with a group of fellow monks in India, they came upon a burning building that was part of a Roman Catholic convent. Several nuns were trapped inside and were shouting for help. Jain monks are strictly forbidden to touch a woman, because so doing is a violation of their religious doctrine and is seen as detrimental to spiritual development. Gurudev Chitrabhanuji realized that ahimsa was the highest law. He ran into the building repeatedly and succeeded in carrying out three of the nuns before being injured by a falling beam.

Non-cooperation

Non-cooperation involves respectful disobedience to an unjust law or command. Examples of non-cooperation can include refusing to participate in military service or the draft, strikes, peaceful occupations of property, or refusing to pay a tax that will finance war. Gandhi wrote:

> Non-cooperation is a protest against an unwitting and unwilling participation in evil... Non-cooperation with an evil is as much a duty as cooperation with good. There is no instrument so clean, so harmless, and yet so effective as non-cooperation.

Pure intent is essential for these more radical expressions of dynamic compassion. Since the true impact of compassion is directly in proportion to our underlying intent for practicing it, we must be very honest with ourselves about our motivations. Ulterior motives of self-gratification, the desire to manipulate others, to achieve publicity for our cause, or dividing people from each other can easily destroy the fragile essence of compassion, and produce only hollow, confusing or temporary results.

At the same time, common sense is essential for nonviolent action, which should be based on a careful analysis of the situation at hand, weighing all of the possibilities, limitations and alternatives. Only then can an aspirant to ahimsa make a sensible judgment according to his or her abilities, knowing that a nonviolent solution may not always be possible.

Injuring or killing an armed attacker as a last resort in order to save the life of another can be a true act of compassion. The heroes who tried to wrest control of United Airlines flight 186 from armed hijackers on September 11, 2001 were motivated by the desire to save the lives of both passengers and those on the ground, even if they were forced to take the lives of the terrorists in the process. Gandhi taught that "Ahimsa is the highest duty. Even if we cannot practice it in full, we must try to understand its spirit and refrain as far as humanly possible from violence."

Dynamic Compassion

Dynamic compassion is by far the most applicable in our daily lives, and thus offers the widest range of opportunities for creative expression. Dynamic compassion does not only call for renouncing himsa where it is usually expressed, but calls upon us to utilize loving, healing and unifying action in all circumstances. This would involve:

-Healing instead of causing harm.
-Respecting and furthering life instead of limiting or destroying it.
-Serving as an active channel for compassion by opening the heart.

As seen in the chart on the following page, this aspect of ahimsa can be expressed on a personal level in our relationships with other people, other species of animals, as well as with plants and minerals. It is reflected on how we conduct our lives inside the home, and how we relate to others as neighbors, businesspeople, teachers and students. It also is reflected by our experience of connectedness with both our local and planetary communities, and the quality of being intimately involved with the world around us. As Matthew Fox, an American priest and theologian best known for reviving the ancient tradition of Creation Spirituality, wrote in *A Spirituality Named Compassion:*

> Compassion is a way of being at home in the universe, with life and with death, with the seen and unseen. The energy-consciousness that com-passion presumes takes one beyond mere psychologies and spiritualities of inter-personalism.

The spirit of dynamic compassion is based on the unitive quality of nature. It can be seen in the cooperative structure of the atom, the symbiotic relationship among plants, soil, water and air; the social quality among humans and other animal species, and the magnetic forces that maintain the delicate balance of the solar system. Magnetism, cooperation, and unity are basic to life and are essential for planetary survival. They are fundamental for all growth and development.

Dynamic compassion can take many forms, and can be integrated and applied in all facets of daily life. It may be true that dynamic compassion is not for the few. It is an innate quality found in every woman, man and child, and is within the reach of everyone who sincerely desires to claim it.

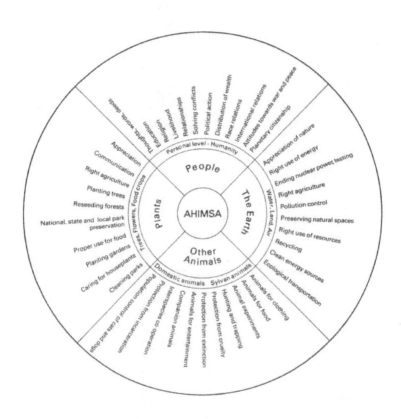

The Scope of Ahimsa

Chapter 2

The Threefold Peace

*Ahimsa, though a negative term, is full of
positive meaning, extending from a simple
act of kindness to a comprehensive outlook
of universal fraternity, and for guiding the
search for the adoption of practical steps
towards realization of universal
brotherhood.*

– Gurudev Chitrabhanuji

THE BASIC FOUNDATION OF ahimsa is composed of
three essential aspects. The first aspect declares that
human beings are fundamentally good. The second speaks
of a universe that is essentially benign and a planet that is
both a safe and nurturing place in which to live. The third
aspect speaks of the immense power of truth and
compassion, and how each individual can make an
important contribution to the overall peace picture.

1. Human beings are fundamentally good

The first aspect is based on the age-old teachings that each individual possesses a spiritual essence or core. As the principle of conscious life which animates our being, it has been referred to as the Christ Within, the Higher Self, and the *atman*. As the core of our being, this higher self contains the essence of love, compassion, truth and wisdom that not only leads us to understand our true task in life, but can help us understand the essence of right relationship and ensure our continued survival on this planet.

Gandhi claimed that this "soul force" is the essence of ahimsa, and is therefore imperishable, changeless and eternal. He refuted the theory that human beings are violent by nature, and wrote, "It is the law of love that rules mankind. Had violence, i.e. hate, ruled us, we should have become extinct long ago." He believed that by getting in touch with our inner spiritual essence, we would better understand our true nature. From a point of this deep place of security and wisdom, we could in turn create a new and more peaceful world.

It is important to remember that his teachings on ahimsa acknowledge our violent side. Like many psychologists and sociologists, Gandhi felt that violence and cruelty are forms of acquired rather than instinctual behavior. While we desperately need to explore the issues behind human cruelty, dishonesty and violence, we must remember above all that our inner essence is holy, wise and compassionate.

Much has been written about the subject of human violence cruelty and evil. Traditional Christian teachings hold that while each of us possesses a human soul or spark of God, evil is an intrinsic part of human nature. We are taught that good and evil are two forces that are diametrically opposed to each other, with each fighting for

17

control. Other philosophies teach a contrary idea, and proclaim that evil is an illusory figment of the imagination and in reality does not exist. Early Native American teachings tend to minimize the existence of evil, and speak instead of balance, of harmony or disharmony. Evil is seen essentially as an extreme imbalance, which can be corrected by returning to the primary laws of the universe as revealed by Nature.

There are many theories about the beginnings of evil and how it manifests in our lives, and numerous books on the subject have been written by psychologists, sociologists and theologians. Several of these books are included in the Bibliography and can be consulted for further study.

However, from a standpoint of ahimsa, evil is considered as a symptom of a problem rather than an essential aspect of our being. One radical idea, often not considered by religious teachers and philosophers, is that evil is essentially the product of numbing or cutting ourselves off from our primary heart feelings rather than as a basic defect in human make-up.

Psychologists point out that when a young child feels hurt or rejected, the numbing of feelings is a primary protection against pain, suffering and humiliation. After repeated hurts, the psychological numbing eventually becomes second nature, and can be maintained long after the original circumstances have changed.

If we look into certain events of our childhood, we can often observe the beginnings of this process very clearly. Some of us may remember a particular event, such as a beating, punishment or act of betrayal on the part of a parent or other trusted adult. It may have been an accident that involved a painful sequence of medical treatments, or witnessing a violent injury or death. Although painful, most of us can remember at least one such experience involving our own emotional or physical pain which could have lead to an inner decision of psychic numbing as a protection from that pain.

In addition to protecting oneself from hurtful outside events, numbing can also defend us from certain inner feelings and impulses we experience as children that we feel uncomfortable about. Sexual feelings, expressions of extreme joy or sadness, anger, pain and neediness are often impulses which we learn to repress at an early age. As a result, we often substitute other types of behavior that are more acceptable to both ourselves and the adults in our lives. Over the years, this numbing substitution reaction becomes an automatic response that is strengthened until we build a wall against our own deeper feelings and instincts.

This numbing and insensitivity towards our own pain can create similar numbing and insensitivity towards the pain of others. In her lecture dealing with the question of evil, Eva Pierrakos, co-founder of a spiritual community known as the Pathwork, observed that "the first spontaneous reaction to others is a feeling for and with them, a compassion or empathy, a participation of the soul. But the second reaction restricts this emotional flow . . . the result is a protective layer of unfeelingness."

She also outlined the three stages of numbness which lay the groundwork for evil. The first stage is a numbness towards the self as a protective mechanism. The second stage is numbness towards others, which is often manifested as a passive attitude of indifference. This stage is perhaps the most pervasive expression of evil where people are simply not affected by the suffering of others. The third and perhaps most outwardly destructive stage is the active inflicting of cruelty, whether by word or deed, omission or commission. It stems from an inability to cope with pent-up rage, the perceived fear of others, or as an advanced process of the protective numbing described earlier.

As most of us have observed in our own lives, the borderline between passive numbing and the active inflicting of cruelty is very thin and precarious, and can often be touched off by outer events and circumstances. Later on in this book we will examine the currents of evil more closely, and will explore ways to transform them.

For an aspirant to a life of ahimsa, the dynamics of evil are very important to understand, not just intellectually, but on the deepest personal levels. Unless we understand that evil (as well as violence, competition and cruelty) is essentially a human choice over which we have personal control, it will continue to wield tremendous power in our lives. By understanding how evil works in our daily lives- and by working to transform its energy- evil will cease to cause so much pain, confusion and despair on both individual and planetary levels.

Understanding Human Nature

A noted psychologist once wrote that the human mind is a complex and amazing thing. There is some truth to his opinion. We humans have the ability to live in different states of reality, which can vary from each other tremendously.

On one hand, we have an often childlike side that always thinks of itself. This side is often vain, selfish, opinionated and destructive. Its time frame is confined to the here and now, not unlike a spoiled (but perhaps likeable) child whose needs demand their parents' immediate attention. While this part of ourselves can often get us into trouble, it also makes our life more interesting. Spiritual teachers have called this part of is the "lower self," which looks out for its interests and wants to have its own way at any cost.

We also have another side to our nature that is known variously as the universal self, the higher self, or the "spark of God within" mentioned earlier. More quiet and subtle than the lower self, it possesses superior wisdom, love and strength that are inclusive, compassionate and ageless. Sometimes we are lucky enough to know an older, wise person who has lived their life and is a source of common sense, practical wisdom and infinite patience. This person accepts us the way we are without judgment, and are happy to offer counsel, which is always wise and helpful. Such an elder is a source of calm and stability in an often crazy world. The higher self is not unlike that special person. No matter what time of the day or night, or wherever we happen to be, we can go there for comfort, wisdom and inspiration.

Peace Pilgrim, who walked over 25,000 miles from 1953 to 1981 through the United States and Canada teaching about peace, spoke about these important aspects of our nature and the need to work with them wisely:

> Your lower self sees things from the
> viewpoint of your physical well-being only-
> your higher self considers your psychological
> or spiritual well-being. Your lower self sees
> you as the center of the universe-your higher
> self sees you as a cell in the body of humanity.
> When you are governed by your lower self
> you are selfish and materialistic, but insofar
> as you follow the promptings of your higher
> self you will see things realistically and feel
> harmony within yourself and others.

In addition to the higher self and the lower self, we also possess the will and knowledge of the mind. Whether it comes to achieving inner peace or peace in the world, working with this part of our makeup can help us achieve several important goals:

1. It allows us to observe the childlike destructive side of ourselves and see how it lives its daily life through attitudes, ideas, fears, emotions and activities that cause us conflicts, keep us separate from others, undermines our happiness, and prevents us from being integrated and whole human beings.

2. At the same time, it can open us to the universal, unlimited part of our being. This not only allows us to contact deeper realities, but enables us to confront and eventually transform negative currents that make us anxious, fearful, angry and generally unhappy.

3. Rather than make us holy, coming into contact with our higher self helps us realize that we are *already holy*: it enables us to see more clearly who we already are as humane beings.

2. The Universe is essentially benign. The Earth is a safe and nurturing home.

Many of us- especially those who live in large cities- experience a degree of insecurity and even fear in relation to our environment, and often feel that the world is s strange and even hostile place in which to live. Some people experience feelings of absolute terror as the prospect of being alone in the forest, or feel uncomfortable in a natural setting without a book, tablet or smart phone to hold their attention. We are especially fearful of earth events like storms, droughts or earthquakes, especially when they cause human death or property damage to our community. Such fears are often justified.

In earlier times, human beings were very much a part of their environment, and lived very close to the land. Many indigenous societies, including all of the early Native

American nations, considered themselves to be an essential part of Nature rather than merely as guests. Their teachings revealed that the Earth is our "Mother", and that we are all closely related to all of the Earth's "children" including other humans, the four-legged and winged animals, plants, streams and even rocks.

This intimate contact with the land produced a physical, mental and emotional state of groundedness that often led to a state of harmony with the environment. According to Native American tradition, this groundedness and sensitivity to one's natural surroundings opened one up to the Greater Mysteries and to the possibility of mystical learning experiences, considered the only way to grasp certain intangible laws of the universe.

It is interesting to note that some of the greatest exponents of ahimsa- including Saint Francis, Henry David Thoreau, Mahatma Gandhi, Dorothy Day, Albert Schweitzer and Peace Pilgrim- were all deeply connected to the land and felt s strong affinity towards other animals and plants. For them, the land was not only a source of food and shelter. It was also a place that offered wisdom and inspired them to deepen their compassion towards all life.

Over the years, as human societies have become more "civilized," we have moved further and further away from the land. We have settled in cities and towns where our environment is artificially controlled as much as possible. This is true even in rural areas where there is still a degree of detachment from the natural world through electricity, air-conditioning, herbicides, lawn mowers, television and computers. This is a fact of modern civilization.

The result of cutting ourselves off from the land has led to a state that body-oriented psychologists call *ungroundedness*. In addition to the actual feeling of detachment from the land, we have also been cut off from our innate "animal" consciousness, which often deprives us of the wisdom and inner security we may have experienced in generations past. The result of this ungrounded state is often insecurity and fear, which leads in turn - as in a vicious cycle - towards a certain degree of numbing towards the natural world around us. Over the years, Nature has been viewed more as an adversary to be defended against, controlled, exploited and abused. Rather than being regarded as a nurturing mother, the Earth has become an economic commodity to do with as we wish.

When we as a society lose our grounding, our collective energy goes frequently from a place of compassion and inner wisdom towards the cold, rational mind. This rational approach to life often traps us (both individually and collectively) in compulsive patterns involving greed, status, indifference and competition as we try to find substitutes for the security we have lost by not being grounded. Wealth addiction, the quest for appearance values, and the desire to dominate others can be traced to this fear of being ungrounded.

Not only has this attitude led to the relentless accumulation of material goods in pursuit of security, but it has also led to a disregard and even contempt towards the so-called four kingdoms - animal, plant, mineral and human - which make up our world. The destruction of forests and other land areas for short-term profit, acid rain, air and water pollution, and toxic waste dumps are among the more obvious examples.

Unfortunately, most people have trouble seeing the connection between our abuses towards the earth and the natural reactions that must follow. During the last century in north-eastern Brazil, for example, vast forests were devastated after it was found that hardwood exports to Europe could bring speculators handsome profits. The large-scale deforestation eventually altered rainfall patterns, which left the entire region subject to severe droughts. Today, the once lush "Nordeste" is the poorest region of the country, where drought, starvation and suffering are commonplace.

When we abuse the land through deforestation, pollution, overgrazing, and the consumption of what we call "our natural resources," native peoples warn that we expose ourselves to the Earth's response. As in a vicious cycle, the movements of Earth towards a natural state of balance (such as drought, storms or earthquakes) make us even more afraid, ungrounded and insecure.

Despite these changes, the Earth Mother still provides for us. The land offers a rich abundance of crops in amazing variety. If generosity and compassion ruled human affairs, fair distribution of this bounty could provide every child, woman and man on the planet with more than enough food to eat. As children of the Earth, we are surrounded by extraordinary beauty in the forms of mountains, lakes, rivers, seashore and sunsets. Because of technological advances, we have the ability to live in harmony with the changes of seasons, and can protect ourselves from excessive sun and storm.

Many of the environmental problems that face humanity, such as droughts, floods and severe weather changes, have their roots in human failings. Ecologists have seen the link between intensive farming and grazing with soil erosion and floods. Deforestation, as earlier described, has been linked to altered weather patterns and droughts. Pollution from motor vehicles and factories has been connected to acid rain, abnormal temperature inversions, and the gradual disappearance of the ozone layer, which protects the Earth's inhabitants from harmful ultra-violet rays. In 2014, the Intergovernmental Panel on Climate Change (IPCC) reported that scientists were more than 95 percent certain that global warming is mostly being caused by human activities, mostly connected to the burning of fossil fuels. This has caused increasing concentrations of greenhouse gases like methane and carbon dioxide (CO_2). It is estimated that about half of the carbon dioxide released from the burning of fossil fuels remains in the atmosphere.

By the same token, there is also ample evidence that when we respect the planet, it will respond in kind. In 1960, Lake Erie was considered biologically dead after being subjected to decades of pollution from factories and municipal sewage. After vigorous efforts were made to stop this pollution, the lake's natural self-cleansing ability was able to function once more, and the lake recovered. As a living body, the Earth will naturally heal itself and do what it can to survive.

While acknowledging the tremendous environmental challenges that confront the planet and especially its human inhabitants, teachers of ahimsa stress the need to return to the innate, "natural" wisdom that each of us possesses. As responsible and caring stewards of the land, we can learn how to live on this planet with an attitude of respect for the other planetary citizens that share the Earth with us. In the third section of this book we will show how returning to a more grounded natural state will enable us to better understand Earth wisdom and planetary movements. We would then be able to live in harmony with our natural environment once more.

3. Truth and compassion are extremely powerful. Each individual can make an important contribution to the overall peace picture.

One of the most troublesome obstacles to a life devoted to ahimsa is the image that our personal power is minimal and that the quality of our daily life has little impact on the outer world. Many of us have been taught to believe that we are each independent entities, and that life is experienced in isolated, watertight compartments. Therefore, the way that we conduct our daily lives does not have a significant impact on the society in which we live.

In reality, however, our effect on others is far greater than we realize. Most of us have, every day, some form of contact with between fifty and a hundred people, whether at work, school, while shopping, or visiting friends or family. When viewed in this context, a negative thought, a careless word, or a selfish action can have a strong potential for causing harm to others. In many cases, people we encounter may respond to a negative expression, and, like a chain reaction, can spread their own hurtful energy to others during the course of the day. Within a matter of hours, one cruel or thoughtless word on the part of one individual can affect - to one degree or another - many dozens of others, just as a stone thrown into a pool will affect every molecule of water in that pool.

Probably most of us are daily the source of perhaps a dozen thoughts, words, or actions which bring about some form of disharmony in our environment. When we multiply this by the number of people in one office, or one school, or one neighborhood or one city, we can see how this daily accumulation of disharmony can add to the total store of accumulated discord in the world. For this reason, the quality of our relationships - both with ourselves and with others - is of tremendous importance. Just as a thousand acts of disharmony can produce mistrust, sorrow and violence, a thousand acts of compassion can add to the healing of the community and ultimately the planet itself. According to Abraham Isaac Kook, one of the most celebrated rabbis of the twentieth century:

> With every moral improvement, with every
> good attribute, every worthwhile subject of
> study, every good deed, even the smallest,

even a goodly conversation, one raises his
own spiritual state; and automatically when
one part of existence rises to a higher state,
all existence is uplifted.

Rabbi Kook was aware of how thought alone can
affect humanity as a whole. This idea was later referred to
by Ken Keyes, Jr., in his book *The Hundredth Monkey:*

When a certain critical number achieves an
awareness, this new awareness may be
communicated from mind to mind. Although
the exact number may vary, the Hundredth
Monkey Phenomenon means that when only
a limited number of people know of a new
way, it may remain the consciousness
property of these people.
 But if there is a point at which if only
one more person tunes in to a new
awareness, a field is strengthened so that this
awareness reaches almost everyone!

The concept that the efforts of a few can have a
major impact on the world was recently discussed in
Malcolm Gladwell's celebrated book, *The Tipping Point:
How Little Things can Make a Big Difference.* According
to Gladwell:

The tipping point is that magic moment when
an idea, trend, or social behavior crosses a
threshold, tips, and spreads like wildfire. Just
as a single sick person can start an epidemic
of the flu, so too can a small but precisely
targeted push cause a fashion trend, the
popularity of a new product, or a drop in the
crime rate.

By transforming our own consciousness, we will be helping to transform the consciousness of humanity. Even if five, ten or fifteen percent of the population begin to envision world peace and send out thoughts of harmony, cooperation and goodwill to the world on a regular basis, a "cosmic shift" can occur in the minds and hearts of the rest of the human family.

The Power Lies Within

Many of us have been indoctrinated by organized religion, the government and especially the media to believe that true power rests outside of ourselves. We rely on religious figures to teach us about morality, we depend on Madison Avenue to determine what we will be wearing next year, and we rely on professional politicians to put an end to global warming or the threat of nuclear war. Teachers of ahimsa believe that true power lies within, and that each of us is capable of tapping into our inner wisdom and strength to make lasting changes both within, and in our relationship to the outer world.

This power can be utilized to create harmony within by giving up smoking or another debilitating habit. It can be used to take better care of our houseplants, our garden or the trees that line our streets. It can be harnessed to relinquish a grudge we've been harboring towards a family member or friend. It may involve picking up bottles or cans that have been thrown on the sidewalk or in a local park. It might entail speaking up for someone who has been maligned by another, or running an errand for a sick friend or neighbor. Some people may choose to write letters or place phone calls to their elected representatives in government, offering praise or constructive criticism as needed. Others may use this power to contribute money to a local environmental group, or perform volunteer work for animal rights or in defense of the homeless.

By working with small things from an inner place of truth, clarity and compassion, we can begin to reclaim our personal power, and play our part in transforming the world around us. Even though our efforts may never be recognized by the public, the accumulated power of our individual thoughts and deeds can be considerable, and can help stem the tide of himsa in the world in favor of true planetary healing. On a simple grassroots level, true personal empowerment can reflect the dynamic essence of ahimsa.

Part II

Ahimsa Among People

Chapter 3

Ahimsa and Right Relationship

Each acts upon others invariably in ways to increase or diminish his own joys and sorrows, depending on whether his action follows the laws of unity which constitute the good and the beautiful, or the ways of separateness which ever cause distortion and conflict.

-N. Sri Ram

THE STATE OF THE WORLD is the sum total of the quality of our relationships. As opposed to a state of isolation, relationship is a dynamic and flowing state of being. It contains the seeds of action, communication and intimacy with others. For this reason, the earliest teachers of ahimsa stressed that the quality of our relationships with each other- whether at home, at school, in the workplace or in social gatherings- is of tremendous importance. Right relationship can help lay the foundation for both individual and planetary transformation.

The philosopher and theosophist Gottfried de Puruker wrote the each one of us is responsible for an aeonic chain of causation, and we cannot speak or act without affecting others. As with a chemical reaction, every one of our thoughts, words and deeds will produce a result that will affect another, for better or worse. When we relate to another person, our level of sensitivity, good intent, generosity, caring and truthfulness will help determine what the effect of our interaction will be. Whether we are a catalyst for pain or discord, or if we contribute to harmony and balance is largely up to us.

The earliest teachers of ahimsa stressed that the quality of our relationships with each other is primarily related to our level of self-understanding. That is why many who have chosen the path of ahimsa to develop the more contemplative side of their nature, and explore the often hidden areas of the psyche and spirit that most people would rather avoid. Discovering and coming to terms with destructive currents, as well as coming upon sources of insight and inner wisdom are seen as essential for the true understanding of what contributes to right relationship. From these inner sources of clarity and strength, we can better manifest ahimsic thoughts, words and deeds in the outer world. This symbolic movement of the incoming tide and the outgoing tide has long been considered essential if we are to live a life of balance and inner centeredness.

Because we have the power to sow the seeds of war and peace in our daily lives, the need to understand the essence of right relationship is extremely important. According to author John L. Hoff in his essay "Practical Friendship":

> We need to know how to build relationship
> and how to use that field of force as an energy

to nurture and guide us - it is our primary resource for human evolution and spiritual development. It is in relationships that we collaborate with each other to create a better world.

Laying the foundation for right relationship is not an easy task. As with any radical act of transformation, it often involves tremendous courage and the desire to confront our most cherished beliefs and images about both ourselves and others, let alone the way we interact with them. It also calls for relinquishing ways of being and modes of behavior (such as
aloofness, aggression or boastfulness) which we have relied on for years in order to function "successfully" in the world.

Separateness and Unity

One of the key concepts integral to ahimsa is that of "feeling with". The ability to empathize with others does not only imply feeling pity or sorrow for them, but a true feeling of identification with others to the degree that it penetrates to the core of our being. For many of us, this act of empathy occurs only on rare occasions. While we may occasionally identify with another person's deep sorrow (especially in the event of a major tragedy) we basically perceive our lives - and those of others - as individual, isolated units. In addition to feeling separate on a physical level, we often believe that nobody but us can experience a particular pain, insight or experience the way we do ourselves. While most of us may feel a shared sorrow when a beloved public figure is murdered or if a group of astronauts perish in an explosion, we often do not identify with the joy, the love, the sorrow, the loneliness or even the cruelty experienced by other human beings on an everyday level. While we may relate to their struggles, triumphs and conflicts at an intellectual level, this idea of "feeling with" rarely penetrates to deeper levels of our being.

Racism

In many societies in the world, racism is a major underlying cause of conflict among people. In a country like the United States- that has a long history of slavery and racial inequality- racism has had a profound negative effect on economic opportunities, housing, access to education, health care and other human rights. As a result, it lays the foundation for conflict and violence.

Racism has classically been defined (mostly by whites) as prejudice against someone based on their skin color or ethnicity. Although prejudice can certainly be an element of racism, a more contemporary definition of racism involves *prejudice plus power*. Like institutionalized himsa, racism is largely institutionalized: in business, housing, law enforcement, the justice system and the schools. For example, those living in minority neighborhoods do not have equal access to housing loans as those living in white neighborhoods do. Schools in poor ("minority") urban neighborhoods are often far inferior to those in white suburbs. People of color are much more likely to be brutalized by the police than those whose skin is white, let alone suffer from a much higher rate of incarceration- especially long-term incarceration- than white people found guilty of similar crimes.

While advances have taken place to further civil rights in the United States, racial discrimination continues to exist in both obvious and more in subtle ways. Nonwhite male motorists are often stopped more by police than white drivers. Available apartments may be suddenly rented by the time a nonwhite family arrives to view them. A Latina woman enters a store waiting to be served, but the employees ignore her, and continue to focus on their cell phones or do paperwork. Yet when a white woman enters the store, the employees immediately wait on her. They may decide to help the Latina only after they take care of her white counterpart.

Although much racial stereotyping has been perpetuated by the media, history books and government, racist ideas are often passed down from parents to children. For an aspirant to a life of ahimsa, uncovering one's own racial privilege and personal racial prejudices-however subtle- is not an easy task. Even Mahatma Gandhi expressed racist views towards black Africans when he was young, and fought to rid himself of racial prejudice as he matured.

Jane Elliot, an anti-racism activist and forerunner of diversity training, is best known for her "Blue Eyes – Brown Eyes" group exercise, in which students with brown eyes are treated well and receive privileges, while those with blue eyes are treated disdainfully and given various impediments. In a much-watched interview on *Al Jazeera*, Ms. Elliot spoke informally yet eloquently of the need for each of us to remove the roots of racial prejudice from our psyche:

> We hate because we've been taught to hate.
> We hate because we're ignorant. We are the
> product of ignorant people who have been
> taught an ignorant thing that there are four
> or five different races. There are not four or
> five different races; there is only one race on
> the face of the Earth and we are all members
> of that race, the human race. But we have
> separated people into races so that some of us
> can see that we are superior to others.

We thought that that would work, I guess, but it hasn't worked. It has been bad for everyone...

There is no gene for racism. There is no gene for bigotry. You are not born a bigot: you have to learn to be a bigot. Anything you learn, you can unlearn. It's time to unlearn our bigotry. It's time to get over this thing and we'd best get over it pretty soon.

I'm an educator. And it's my business as an educator to lead people out of ignorance: the ignorance of thinking that you are better or worse than someone else because of the amount of pigment in your skin. Pigmentation has nothing to do with intelligence or with your worth as a human being. It's time to get over that!

Feeling Special

Like beliefs surrounding race, the sensation of feeling "special" or separate from others can be traced to our earliest childhood. Many of us competed with our siblings for our parents' attention and affection with the hope of being the favorite son or daughter. For children without brothers or sisters, being the favorite was a given. As we grew older, these narcissistic images were reinforced in school, where we learned the importance of being the most attractive, the most popular, the coolest or the most athletic. When we observe modern society, we find that narcissism has become a prominent feature in our interactions on social media ("I am special. Look at me!") along with our obsession with status, appearance values and celebrities.

The dominant system of education is based on competition, standing out from others, and the belief that the student's primary goal is to become a productive citizen who will conform to the establish order. Memorization, grade point averages, intelligence tests, SAT scores and college percentile rankings all help lay the groundwork for one's future life "out in the real world".

For the most part, this early training helps strengthen an inherently violent and antiquated school system where the rule is "every man/woman for himself/herself". It is a world where competition, freed and personal ambition govern the conduct of human relationships. In such a world, other human beings are viewed primarily as a means to fulfilling our personal goals and are thus objects to be manipulated or exploited by subtle or not-so-subtle means. Whether we are speaking of a landlord evicting all her poor or elderly tenants in order to increase her profits, or of a man being extra charming in order to seduce his date, the feeling of separateness and self-centeredness is the same. Despite recent discoveries in physics, biology, astronomy and mathematics that point to the unitive nature of the universe and the interrelationship of all life on Earth, many still cling to the old concepts of a separatist world-view, which concentrates on fragmentation and differentiation of people and other forms of life.

Adopting a unitive view of the world does not mean that we cannot appreciate the remarkable diversity in our vast human community. Whether we visit people in a faraway country, or merely explore the differences that exist among members of a single household, we can readily observe a range of customs, habits, emotions, tastes and beliefs that add to the complexity and beauty of what being a human being is all about.

Yet on a deeper level that goes beyond appearances, we need to see how intimately related we are as human beings on physical, emotional and spiritual levels. We all share the capacity to experience deep joy or sorrow, and harbor the potential for violence as well as that of caring for and nurturing others. We are ruled by the same biological laws and all require nourishment, oxygen, rest, affection and shelter. No matter what religion we profess, whatever language we speak, or whatever color our skin may be, we have far more in common with each other than not.

The earliest teachers of ahimsa believed that recognizing our essential unity with the rest of humanity is the first step towards nonviolence, and lays the foundation for a new kind of human relationship which can eventually transform the world. According to the Tibetan lama Tarthang Tulku:

> Once we recognize all that we have in
> common with others, a feeling of compassion
> naturally arises and we can no longer treat
> other people with such indifference. We more
> easily understand their problems, and as we
> learn to heal ourselves, we begin to use our
> knowledge to heal them as well.

For many of us, a fundamental longing is to reclaim this lost sense of unity with others; not just with people, but with the whole living world around us. We feel the difficulty of this task, as we have often been conditioned from childhood to believe that the ideal life is one of independence, and that the joys and sorrows of others are not really our own.

Living in the Moment

There is no simple, easy technique for breaking down such barriers, which often requires careful observation and self-awareness. However, some modern teachers of ahimsa have suggested that we try to imagine that whatever feeling we are experiencing *at this moment* is also being felt by thousands, if not millions, of others at the same time throughout the world. Whether this experience involves anger, joy, feeling cut-off, inspiration or jealousy, we need to realize that we are not alone in our experience.

By the same token, when we observe others going through a particular experience, we can consciously learn to relate to their success or their struggle and "feel with" them. Gradually, this deepening and expanding consciousness of others will lead us to enter a state of compassion that will be completely spontaneous and natural.

The process of "opening up" in this way can be painful. As mentioned earlier, cutting off from feelings of sadness, yearning or even intense joy is often an automatic response based on early childhood events. However, the realization that millions of others around the world are also struggling against feeling their pain at the moment can be encouraging and healing in itself.

The ability to "feel with" can also lead us to understand what lies beyond another person's attitudes and actions. We instinctively begin to see others are they really are, free from idealized images of good or evil. The Indian philosopher Haridas Chauduri wrote the naïve faith in the goodness of others leads to a good deal of suffering in their hands. At the same time, universal mistrust of others brings about isolation and spiritual suffocation. He believed that by understanding ourselves on a deep level and confronting those aspects of in us that are dishonest, greedy or manipulative, we can better understand the inner currents that motivate others. This can help us to view others with more clarity and avoid "hooking in" to their negative thoughts and actions. As we interact with them on a more realistic level, we can learn how to be understanding and accommodating towards them without allowing ourselves to be deceived, manipulated or otherwise taken advantage of.

Towards Resolving Conflicts

In any relationship there is bound to be some degree of conflict. Whether as a result of different personalities or different needs, conflicts often occur when two or more people interact with each other.

Contrary to popular belief, conflict is not always negative; in fact, it often has positive aspects. In addition to helping us to focus on what we really want for ourselves or others, we also learn to compromise through conflict and to relinquish what we do not really need. Conflict can often bring people closer together as they work to resolve their differences in a spirit of cooperation and positive intent.

Ahimsa is essential for aiding in conflict resolution. Whether on an interpersonal or international level, a motive grounded in compassion, understanding and goodwill can go far towards resolving conflicts for the highest good of all concerned.

Peace Pilgrim, an extraordinary woman who walked over 25,000 miles throughout North America from 1953 until her death in 1981 spreading the message of peace, wrote that whenever we are in conflict with another person, our primary goal should be to work towards resolving the difficulty rather than gaining the advantage. She taught that when this occurs, a transformation between the persons involved can take place as they enter into a type of collaboration towards the resolution of a common problem. As we begin to view others as partners rather than adversaries, efforts to resolve problems take a different form.

Part of this ahimsic attitude towards conflict resolution involves taking personal responsibility for our

41

role in the conflict or problem. While we may not actually be guilty of an overt act of violence, we may be guilty of committing a more subtle form of himsa which may have contributed to the problem. By showing off, indulging in gossip, putting others down, offering unsolicited and unwelcome advice or criticism, failing to listen or withholding help when needed, we may be expressing the more subtle forms of himsa to others.

Looking Beneath the Surface

In many instances, irrational psychological currents underlie a particular conflict, often adding a powerful emotional "charge" to an otherwise minor problem or disagreement. For that reason, we need to ask ourselves hard questions about the possible role these currents may play in blocking an otherwise amicable resolution to a problem.

Issues of jealousy, competition, fear and holding on to past hurts are some of the most common. We may be especially self-righteous, stubborn and unforgiving when the other person reveals an undesirable trait which we may dislike in ourselves. We often judge ourselves severely for these defects (be they dishonesty, feelings of self-importance or revengefulness) and therefore may direct our wrath towards our adversary.

In some organizations, such as the International Pathwork Foundation, participants are encouraged to express their judgments of others before they even begin to resolve a concrete problem. Often utilizing a rubber bat (bataca) on a pillow to emphasize their statements, people are to expose what are often irrational feelings in a safe and nurturing space. They can also reveal any hidden agendas they may have that have helped prolong or exacerbate the conflict. As everyone involved with the problem works in good faith to explore these issues, he or she can come upon creative ways to resolve the difficulty.

Others utilize a process called psychodrama, where different roles are acted out in order to illustrate certain personality traits or to achieve a better understanding of the other person's position in the situation. In some cases, the opponents may actually switch roles and play each other. From this place of discovery, both parties can resolve the psychological blocks that hinder the resolution of a conflict or problem.

Listening with the Heart

Closely linked with this attitude of creatively resolving conflicts together is listening with the heart. Since traditional methods of negotiation involve trying to convince the other person that we are right, we are often unwilling to sit down and truly listen to the other, without interruption. Listening to another person with an open mind and an open heart opens us to the possibility that we may have much to learn from the other person's point of view and that what he or she says may be true, at least in part.

Taught under various labels (deep listening, receptive listening, compassionate listening) by therapist and peace worker Gene Knudsen Hoffman, the Buddhist monk Thich Nhat Hanh and others, opening the heart and truly listening to another person will not only help alleviate their anger and suffering, but can open the door to conflict resolution, whether at the moment or in the future. Ms. Knudson Hoffman explained the essence of compassionate listening during a talk in California:

> Compassionate listening requires a particular attitude. It is non-judgmental, non-adversarial, and seeks the truth of the person

questioned. It also seeks to see through any masks of hostility and fear to the sacredness of the individual and to discern the wounds suffered by all parties. Listeners do not defend themselves, but accept what others say as their perceptions. By listening, they validate the other's right to their perceptions.

One of the key concepts in compassionate listening is "not judging" and to be receptive to what the other person has to say to us, despite our discomfort. By opening ourselves to the other person, we can utilize deep listening in any conflict situation. Writing in the magazine *Nurse.com West*, Cari L. Allen, a psychiatric nurse from Kansas, addressed the need to truly listen to patients with mental disorders, including those who may be physically aggressive:

> ...Aggression is a way to communicate when all other communication has failed to address fears or meet needs. If we keep that in mind rather than labeling or judging when an individual's behaviors are escalating, we can make strides to break down barriers and facilitate healing.

By moving through our fear, stubbornness and pride, we can begin an honest dialogue with the other person, and provide him or her with the psychological space to be receptive to our viewpoint as well. By working from a foundation of vulnerability and openness, the energy normally used for self-defense and manipulation can be channeled into finding creative solutions to problems so that will not be recreated in the future.

There are many useful approaches to peaceful conflict resolution, but they can be summarized by the following six points:

1. Stay calm. Before beginning the process of conflict resolution, a short period of meditation or prayer will help you to remain grounded and calm. Be especially aware of feelings of anger and frustration as they come up during your interaction so they do not take control.

2. Let the other person speak. Many people simply need to be heard and their thoughts acknowledged. By allowing the other person to finish their thoughts without interruption, you can do much to help defuse a difficult situation.

3. Genuinely consider the other person's point of view. Look for areas of common ground and build on them.

4. Validate the other person. Find areas that you agree with. This will not only show respect for the other person's feelings, but you gradually help to defuse their anger as well.

5. If you are wrong, quickly admit it and take responsibility by offering to make changes in your beliefs or behavior. Admitting that we are wrong takes a lot of courage, but it can quickly change a difficult dynamic between you and others.

6. Look beyond appearances. Rather than view the other person as your opponent, strive to view them as another spiritual being to be acknowledged, loved and validated.

Resolving conflicts peacefully need not involve tremendous effort. But it calls upon us to be aware, humble and open to another's point of view. However, the benefits of resolving a problem through ahimsa are manifold. In addition to resolving the conflict itself, it creates a benign cycle of trust and cooperation, making future difficulties earlier to resolve with less effort. And by working from a position of respect and compassion, all participants involved in resolving the conflict are nurtured and healed.

Ahimsa and Truth

One of the major obstacles to right relationship is the tendency not to be in truth. Lying has reached truly epidemic proportions in our society. Dishonesty is not only practiced in our personal relationships, but is routine practice in business, in religious life, and especially in the media and in politics.

The modern phenomenon of "fake news" that played a powerful role in the United States presidential election in 2016 has impacted millions of people through social media outlets like Facebook, Twitter and Buzzfeed. The goal of the purveyors of fake news is to spread stories that are patently false to a largely passive audience that tends to believe whatever they read.

Writing in billmoyers.com., journalist Neal Gabler warned that fake news "is not intended to pose an alternative truth, as if there could be such a thing, but to destroy truth altogether, to set us adrift in a world of belief without facts, a world where there is no defense against lies. That, needless to say, is a very dangerous place."

Of course, truth- even in the mainstream media- has often been insufficiently and carelessly applied. A 2012 Gallup poll found that Americans' distrust in the mainstream media was higher than it had ever been, with 60 percent saying they had little or no trust in the mass media to report the news fully, accurately, and fairly. This percentage has likely increased in recent years.

The news media are a business and not a public service. A large part of that business is providing what the public wants, focusing on celebrity gossip, the latest fashion trends and political sound bites rather than in-depth analysis of important issues that shape our lives.

This reality poses a major challenge to seekers of truth, because almost every news article must be carefully scrutinized and evaluated. Many news articles are intended to instill fear, confusion, paranoia and hopelessness. Sources need to be checked and the consumer of news must be vigilant to look at the underlying reasons why the information is being disseminated and whether it is based on fact or fiction. Since many of us who watch, read or listen to the news tend to be passive, motivating ourselves to distinguish falsehood from truth is not an easy task.

Lying: A Worldwide Pandemic

In his popular book *Lying*, neuroscientist Sam Harris maintains that most forms of private vice and public evil are kindled and sustained by lies. Acts of adultery and other personal betrayals, financial fraud, government corruption—including murder and genocide—often require an additional moral defect: a willingness to lie.

An 2016 article in *The New Yorker* magazine mentioned that according to psychologist Robert Feldman, we lie an average of three times during a routine ten-minute conversation with a stranger or casual acquaintance. Hardly anyone refrains from lying altogether, and some people report lying up to twelve times within that time span. The price we pay for untruthfulness is very high. When people are unable to trust others, the fabric of society is weakened. Confusion, instability and violence often result.

Ever since the philosophy of ahimsa came into being, its cardinal virtues have been those of compassion and truth. The Jains, whose religious beliefs are founded on ahimsa, consider falsehood to be a major violation of cosmic law and must be guarded against at all times. Over the centuries, the Jains classified hundreds of types of false statements that fell into three main categories. Placed in a contemporary context, they are as follows:

1. Statements that falsely refer to an object's position, time and nature, such as "John is not here" when in fact, he is.

2. Statements that claim that a thing exists where it does not exist, such as "The check is in the mail."

3. Statements that represent an existing thing as something different than it really is, such as "This is a priceless antique" when in reality it is a copy.

The Jains further defined falsehood as encompassing

1. "Condemnable" speech, which included backbiting, harshness, unsuitable comments, nonsense, or telling offensive jokes;

2. Speech that induces another person to engage in injuring other living beings; and

3. Any speech that causes uneasiness, fear, pain, hostility, grief or mental anguish.

In addition to gossip and backbiting, Dayanand Bhargava, the author of *Jaina Ethics* suggests that when adhering to truth, one's speech should aim for moderation rather than exaggeration, esteem rather than degradation, and distinction rather than vulgarity. He continues:

All untruth necessarily involves violence for it is caused by negligence, which is the backbone of violence. It is, therefore, unthoughtful speech, anger, greed, fear and cutting of jokes which should be avoided to protect the vow of truthfulness.

Why Lie?

There are many reasons for choosing not to be in truth. For many people, lying (whether it be in the form of an outright untruth, exaggeration, understatement, omission, or the famous "white lie") is routinely used to manipulate the feelings and thoughts of others, especially in business, politics and the media, including websites, blogs and social media. Lying is also used to defend us when we are confronted, and helps us to avoid being held accountable for our actions. Lying is often essential in the selling of goods and services, and frequently encourages people to buy what they do not need.

Trying to appear younger, older, more sophisticated or more intelligent are also forms of untruthfulness, as is hiding one's true feelings behind a mask of humility, submissiveness, machismo, kindness or feigned interest.

In certain cases, untruth may be a legitimate tool to defend ourselves or another person from harm. Those who protected Jews from the Nazis during World War Two often lied to Nazi soldiers in order to save their Jewish friends from the concentration camps. While not totally in harmony with ahimsa, the motive behind the rare expression of untruth needs to be taken into account.

The price we pay for dishonesty is high. By living out of truth, we create a split in our beings. On the one hand we know in our hearts what is the truth, while our outer expression is dishonesty, usually rationalized by the mind. This often leads to vicious cycles involving guilt, depression and the inability to trust oneself or others. Whether we attempt to cover up a mistake at work, try to avoid someone we have been dishonest with in the past, or have to remember an old alibi or excuse ("When you tell the truth, there is nothing you have to remember"), our efforts involve tremendous emotional and mental energy. In addition to the toll that untruthfulness takes on our own level of well-being, it creates barriers of suspicion and anger in others that hinder future cooperation.

In many ways, lying is like a cancer that destroys the fabric of society. It erodes both the foundation for healthy human relationships and the essence of what would otherwise be benign public institutions. Despite any short-term benefits that are gained through dishonest words and actions, the long-term results are always destructive.

Honesty: Back to the Essence

Striving towards total honesty in daily life is strongly connected to the goal of ahimsa. Truthfulness vibrates with the very core of our being, as well as with the Higher Self of others. It is the recognition of what is, and is therefore grounded in reality.

While untruth and lying cause fragmentation and help destroy the fragile essence of cooperation and trust, telling the truth, keeping our word, and living a life free from deception are in harmony with the forces of stability, cohesiveness and growth.

However, living a life that is honest and transparent does not mean that we need to reveal intimate details about ourselves or others on social media or to whoever we meet at a social gathering. Nor does it require us to be reckless and insensitive with our observations of others. When considered from an ahimsic point of view, it is often better to say nothing than to use truth and honesty as a means to cause injury or pain to others. In the classic work

At the Feet of the Master, we are advised that if what we have to say is not true, kind *and* helpful, we should remain silent.

Unfortunately, many aspirants to nonviolence tend to take this advice to the extreme: they keep both their feelings and opinions – whether positive or negative- to themselves rather than to risk taking a stand on an issue or confronting another person when the situation calls for it. Some keep silent because they want to avoid an unpleasant confrontation if their views are not perceived as helpful, or they are afraid that some of their own negativity may be expressed while sharing their views.

Yet by withholding from others, we can also be guilty of himsa. As with sharing food, the act of sharing our thoughts and feelings can be a source of nourishment to others. When expressed from a place of kindness and respect, even criticism or negative feelings can have a beneficial effect on others and can help them achieve a deeper level of understanding.

Very often an angry word or negative attitude serves as a defense against a deeper emotion, such as fear or loneliness. By courageously moving through our pride and communicating with the other person directly and honestly, we can give of ourselves in the best sense of the word. As a result, benign cycles of respect, trust and understanding can lay the foundation in our relationships, and can begin - at a grassroots level - to transform the fabric of human society.

Chapter 4

Ahimsa, War and Peace

The choice today is no longer between violence and nonviolence. It is either nonviolence or nonexistence.

-Martin Luther King, Jr.

A NOTED PHILOSOPHER ONCE observed that the history of humanity has been a history of its wars. During the past 5,000 years we have fought over 12,000 wars - approximately two and a half wars every year. With the passing of the seasons we are witness to at least one major war between nations, several domestic guerrilla wars, ongoing terrorist attacks, domestic rioting and other violent manifestations of civil strife.

World War One (1914-1918) was heralded as "the war to end all wars," yet wars have continued to proliferate, and most of us still accept the idea that violence is an acceptable means to settle disputes. In many nations of the world, war is glorified in textbooks, in movies and on television; war toys are given to children at Christmas; war veterans fondly reminisce about their past experiences, which were often the most exciting moments of their lives. Taxpayers willingly spend a large percentage of their hard-earned salaries on missiles, bombs, warplanes and military research.

According to the Stockholm International Peace Research Institute, by 2015 the world military spending reached $1.676 trillion. This corresponds to 2.5 percent of the world's gross domestic product (GDP), or approximately $249 for each person living in the world today. The fifteen countries with the highest spending account for 81 percent of the total. The United States is responsible for 39 percent ($596 billion), followed by China ($215 billion), Saudi Arabia ($87.2 billion), Russia ($66.4 billion) and the United Kingdom ($55.5 billion). All in all, the planetary expenditure for military research and development alone is estimated to be in excess of $60 billion a year.

According to the non-partisan Arms Control Association, the United States and Russia are armed with a combined total of about 9,000 nuclear warheads, plus another 5,000 that are retired but not yet dismantled. At the time of this writing (2017) another thousand or more nuclear warheads belonged to France, the United Kingdom, China, India, Pakistan and Israel. Iran and the Democratic People's Republic of Korea (also known as North Korea) were suspected of having nuclear weapons, but their leaders denied it. At the same time, both the leaders of Russia and the United States called for greatly expanding their nuclear arsenals. In addition to the danger of terrorists stealing nuclear materials from countries like Pakistan and Ukraine, the ACA highlighted the constant threat of nuclear war between nations:

> The threat of nuclear war between the United States and Russia or China, by mistake or miscalculation, has increased due to a general

deterioration of relations and regional tensions over eastern Europe, Ukraine, Syria, and the South and East China seas. Russia dropped out of the nuclear security summit process in 2016, and Moscow and Washington have exchanged charges of violating the 1987 Intermediate-Range Nuclear Forces Treaty, which eliminated an entire class of nuclear weapons.

By 2016, the United States military budget was estimated to be 21 percent of all Federal outlays in 2017, compared with 28 percent for health care, 25 percent for pensions, 3 percent for education and 3 percent for transportation. The United States spends more in one year on the military than the governments of all the developing nations in the world (encompassing some 5.9 billion people) spend on health care.

Doomed to War?

When we consider the subject of war, peace and international relations, many of us experience frustration over the possible alternatives to war and whether or not humanity can be saved. We mentioned earlier that some people maintain that human beings are violent by nature, and therefore war is inevitable. Others claim that God or Nature played a trick with our development, and we are unable to save ourselves from destruction. Some feel that even though we ourselves may desire peace, others do not, so working for peace is an exercise in futility.

Some years ago, Mahatma Gandhi observed that if hate and violence were the laws of mankind, the human race would have become extinct long ago. Although many of the current problems facing humanity may appear insurmountable, Gandhi's belief in the fundamental wisdom of human nature may be justified. How then can the aspirant to ahimsa deal effectively with the present international situation in a manner that would be both beneficial and lasting?

In order to better understand the alternatives to war, we need to shift our focus towards the myriad "benefits" of weapons research and development and how they impact on the total world peace picture. Despite the strong emphasis politicians place on patriotism, freedom and democracy when it comes to supporting military action, the core of the matter is money: the short-term financial gains to be made in a war-orientated economy are enormous, as they have been throughout history. Standing armies, defense systems and the worldwide trade in armaments are a crucial factor in expanding and maintaining a strong traditional economy in any industrialized nation.

United States President Dwight Eisenhower addressed the problem of what he called the "military industrial complex" in a speech given shortly before he left office in 1961. What is perhaps most overlooked is that this speech was given by a celebrated Army general who believed in a strong national defense.

> In the councils of government, we must guard
> against the acquisition of unwarranted
> influence, whether sought or unsought, by
> the military industrial complex. The potential
> for the disastrous rise of misplaced power
> exists and will persist. We must never let the
> weight of this combination endanger our
> liberties or democratic processes. We should
> take nothing for granted. Only an alert and
> knowledgeable citizenry can compel the
> proper meshing of the huge industrial and

military machinery of defense with our
peaceful methods and goals, so that security
and liberty may prosper together.

When we look at the military from a strictly economic standpoint, we see that the armed forces are pure consumers. Totally subsidized by taxpayers, the military consumes a staggering quantity of war material, technical resources, manpower, food, clothing, shelter and energy, especially in the forms of electricity and petroleum. In exchange for nearly $600 billion a year spent on goods and services, the military provides the residents of a country like the United States of America with "protection" in both times of war and times of peace.

This idea of protection from the enemy is essential to the national policy of not only the United States, but also China, Russia, India, Saudi Arabia and most European nations, both East and West. Some feel that when we consider that the world in the nuclear age is but a global village in which all human beings are interrelated and interdependent, the concept of "enemy" is ludicrous, especially when former enemies in past wars are now close friends and trading partners. Nevertheless, the "enemy" is needed in order to maintain the present war-orientated economy.

The American philosopher and futurist William Irwin Thompson spoke to this issue in 1985, when the Cold War with the former Soviet Union was nearing its end: "The Soviet Union is a more important part of America than Maine or North Dakota. We could lose those states and really be fine, but if we lost our enemy, we'd collapse." He based his comment on the belief that if the governments of the Soviet Union and the United States decided to cease all hostilities and co-operate towards a common goal of making the planet safe for humanity, the war-orientated economy of both nations (though especially the United States) would be plunged into a severe crisis.

In a speech presented before the American Bankers' Association, Frank Pace, Jr., former Secretary of the United States Army, spoke of the importance of military spending and its impact on the nation's economy:

> If there is, and I suspect there is, a direct relation between the stimulus of large defense spending and a substantially increased rate of growth of gross national product, it quite simply follows that defense spending *per se* might be countenanced on *economic grounds alone* [italics mine] as a stimulator of the national metabolism.

Big business takes this issue so much to heart, that whenever news came of a possible peace settlement to the Vietnam War in 1970-71, stock markets around the world took a nosedive.

At the present time, millions of jobs are related to the war industry. According to the United States Bureau of Labor Statistics, 76,000 jobs are created for each $1 billion spent on armaments and military research in the USA. Nuclear scientists, space researchers, biologists, geneticists, chemists and engineers work at jobs most closely linked to the war industry. Millions of others - from truck assemblers to button makers - count on military contracts to provide them with work. Making weapons has become a U.S. specialty, with 47 American companies filling the top 100 grossing slots in the world. These companies not only supply the United States Armed Forces, but sell their products to dozens of foreign governments.

Although it cannot be denied that some military research- especially in computer technology, health protection and communication- can benefit the civilian population, military projects like the Aero-Optical Beam Control program, the Excalibur program and the High Energy Liquid Area Defense System (HELLADS) provide universities with lifetime research grants and an assured source of income for decades to come.

Whenever the call goes out for a reduction of the military budget, millions of people become afraid of losing their military-related jobs. This fear is often exploited by politicians and other representatives of the military-industrial complex who warn of weakened defenses and economic collapse if less money is spent on new missiles, weapons, planes and ships. In a sense, this fear is justified, because multinational companies like General Electric and Westinghouse are not surviving by making refrigerators and toaster ovens. In a war-orientated economy, lucrative military contracts are the major source of income for these and similar companies that do not wish to look beyond the short-term benefits such contracts may bring.

Yet, when we examine the long-term results of a war-orientated economy, we can see that the economics of war can lead to disaster. In exchange for the promise of job security, workers are forced to put up with high interest rates, government deficits and their accompanying debt-servicing, inflation, high taxes, the reckless depletion of the Earth's petroleum, minerals, and water resources, and curtailed programs in the areas of health, environmental protection, transportation, education and housing. In addition, the powerful negative influence of the specter of nuclear war on the human psyche - and the feelings of anxiety, fear and hopelessness it engenders - is difficult to calculate in monetary terms. Psychologists say that the present increases in drug addiction, alcoholism and suicide (especially among teenagers) in countries like the United States, Great Britain and Russia may be due in part to the widespread belief that nuclear war is inevitable and that life is of little value.

As with the hydrocarbon engine, government and big business have not seriously committed themselves to exploring alternatives to the present war-orientated economy. When viewed in the short term, stockholders, management and trade unions are very reluctant to risk moving towards a peace-orientated economy, and their unwillingness is strengthened by an apathetic populace, which vaguely shares the belief that the end of military research and production will lead to unemployment and general economic collapse.

The fact is, there are many imaginative alternatives which can take the place of war materials within the framework of the national economy. One rather unorthodox suggestion was introduced by sociologist Philip Slater, who believed that people should be subsidized *not* to produce armaments rather than to produce them:

> I personally would far rather pay people *not*
> to make nerve gas than pay them to make it;
> pay them *not* to pollute the environment than
> pay them to do it. . . pay them *not* to swindle
> us than pay them to do it; pay them *not* to kill
> peasants than pay them to do it. . . One thing
> must be said for idleness: it keeps people
> from doing the Devil's work.

On a more realistic level, a long-term reorientation of commitment can channel enormous talent, resources and energy into areas of need that are often neglected by a war-orientated economy: health, education, public transportation, infrastructure, housing and environmental protection. Aside from the obvious positive impact on the quality of life of those living in such a country, a major reorientation towards a peace-related economy will also stimulate a similar trend in other nations towards improving the quality of life of their own populations. From an economic viewpoint alone, a greater number of jobs can be created in peace-related areas than in those devoted to military research and arms development. The result can be a more diversified, decentralized, enlightened and life-sustaining economic system.

Health

A major reorientation towards a peace economy will bring about an increase in both talent and money in all health-care fields. Essential medical research, education and training facilities will be greatly enhanced. Hospitals, nursing homes, hospices and clinics will be constructed or rehabilitated, and will be better equipped and staffed. Adequate medical and dental care (and especially care geared towards preventive medicine) will be within the reach of every individual free of charge.

According to the United States Bureau of Labor Statistics, 139,000 jobs can be created in this field per $1 billion spent, as opposed to 76,000 jobs devoted to military production. This estimate is valid for countries like the United Kingdom, France, Russia and other industrialized nations as well.

Education

With the freeing up of funds from military development, research and production, a radical improvement in both the level and quality of education can take place. There can be an expansion of educational opportunities for both children and adults. An educational goal equivalent to what is presently considered as a professional degree can be within the reach of all who desire it. Special opportunities can be created for both the handicapped and the elderly.

The construction and/or modernization of schools also would increase, especially in the inner cities and rural areas of the country. New libraries would be constructed, and existing ones can be expanded or modernized, with a greater variety of learning materials and services made available to the public. For each $1 billion spent, approximately 187,000 jobs can be created in the field of education: more than twice as many jobs per $1 billion spent on the military.

Transportation

In a peace-orientated economy, a radical upgrading and expansion of all public transportation systems can take place, so that personal travel on buses, streetcars and railways would be more a pleasure than a necessity. These improvements would work in tandem with the improved maintenance and safety of roads and city streets. Bike paths could become an essential part of every city and town. Funds could also be allocated for the research and development of alternative transportation systems, such as monorail, Maglev (and other light rail systems), hydrofoil and hovercraft vehicles. Airport facilities would also be modernized and improved, with an increase in experienced air-traffic controllers.

Expanded research and development of pollution-free engines and new forms of energy-saving, fuel-efficient cars, trucks and buses can finally be given the attention it deserves. The United States Bureau of Labor Statistics estimated that 92,000 jobs can be created in the transportation sector for each $1 billion spent, which is 21 per cent more than the number of jobs created in a traditional war-orientated economy.

Housing

Clean, comfortable, safe and spacious living accommodation could come within the reach of all through both government-sponsored and private projects. The total elimination of urban slums could finally become a reality, and the city environment could be tailored to a more human scale. There could also be a large-scale rehabilitation of existing housing stock, with improved insulation, plumbing, electric and heating systems.

In addition to better protection from the elements, millions of people would be able to beautify their homes and grounds, with the increased planting of neighborhood gardens and trees. The US Bureau of Labor Statistics estimated that approximately 100,000 jobs could be created per $1 billion spent on the construction and redevelopment of housing and the improvement and care of the surrounding landscape.

Environment

In a peace-orientated economy, more attention will be devoted to protecting the environment and ensuring the wellbeing of all. Increased resources would be directed towards the protection and stewardship of rivers, lakes, oceans, streams, forests and wildlife reserves. Public parks on local, state and national levels could be created and existing parks could be better protected and maintained.

Dynamic efforts would be initiated to eliminate chemical and bacteriological contaminants from the soil, air and water. Active research would be increased to develop alternative sources of clean energy to nuclear power, oil and coal.

Impractical?

Some may feel that these schemes are totally impractical and idealistic, and are beyond the scope of present-day reality. However, students of ahimsa need to envision the possibilities of a peace-directed economy and challenge the old beliefs that preparation for war, larger and more powerful bombs, advanced missile technologies, international tensions, patriotic posturing, espionage, cyber warfare and the constant fear of nuclear holocaust or terrorist attack are in any way "practical." It is clear that after decades of military buildup, national indebtedness, environmental pollution, millions of refugees, and ongoing civil strife there is a need to reassess the idea that a war-orientated economy is "practical" and "realistic" and will lead to the continued security and well-being of the citizens of the Earth.

The transition from an economy that supports the arms race to one which is geared towards peace is not an easy task. As students of ahimsa are aware, the underlying step is a shift in consciousness and the visualization of what *could be* if we choose to pursue it.

Such a change of consciousness led workers at Lucas Aerospace, a British military supplier, to draw up a detailed "Alternative Corporate Plan" as far back as the mid 1970s. This plan suggested socially needed products and services that could be provided by Lucas. Through close co-operation between labor and management, a vast amount of energy, talent and financial resources was channeled into the research and development of new products and services for the civilian market which helped diversify and revitalize the company.

According to a study by a group composed of Swedish workers and managers, prime components for such conversion include an orientation towards high-technology items, a closer connection between technology

63

and civilian products (very often civilian items, such as airplanes, are largely the result of military research), a strengthening of the company's marketing organization towards the civil sector, and a lower level of dependence on all military-related exports.

Like the workers at Lucas, others have the potential to set alternative goals. Workers can act through trade unions to examine their pool of talent and resources. By so doing, they can tap into a wealth of practical ideas for creating technologies that will produce non-military products for the future. If each world citizen, whether a student, a worker, a parent, a teacher, a scientist or a farmer would speak out in favor of alternatives to a war-orientated economy, the impact would be felt in business, in schools and universities, in the media and in the government on both local and national levels.

This would, over time, lead to a clearer understanding of the long- and short-term economic and social costs connected to military preparations, and could lead both corporations and governments to explore the possibilities of directing money formerly spent on the military towards establishing a peace-orientated economy. A defense contractor could be required, for example, to set aside a portion of its profits in a "conversion resource fund" to be released only for non-military purposes.

In many cases, such initiatives would lead to a more equal distribution of technology and resources to those residing and working in poorer nations. This would help reduce the gap between the rich and the poor, and would alleviate a major cause of internal and international conflict. With the ongoing cooperation of business and educational institutions, governments can create the necessary preparations, and, where appropriate, plan to redirect monies freed by disarmament towards meeting urgent economic and social needs of people living both within the country's borders and in other countries as well.

War and militarism are two basic means for tearing down, while ahimsa explores alternatives for survival and growth. If we are to survive on this planet, we need to examine the personal and planetary impact of arms spending, nuclear weapons research, and continued international tensions on our lives. At the same time, we need to examine our personal role in the creation and maintenance of a war-orientated economy, and see how our own beliefs, attitudes and actions can either maintain the status quo or actively work towards peaceful change and planetary survival.

Peace Begins at Home

The goal of world peace through personal transformation has been stressed by many. Mahatma Gandhi believed that if many individuals worked to create peaceful conditions among themselves in daily life, peace among nations would follow as a natural result. Leo Tolstoy stressed that if each person developed his or her own political philosophy, they would not fall prey to propaganda and other conditioning by governments and other institutions.

U Thant, former General Secretary of the United Nations, encouraged a greater personal understanding of the culture and traditions of people of other lands, which would translate into an increased appreciation of their points of view. Albert Einstein and Sir Bertrand Russell urged that the individual learn about the dangers of nuclear war and translate this understanding into actively campaigning for disarmament.

Peace Pilgrim often used letters people wrote to her to illustrate how an individual could promote peace in the world:

One day as I was answering my mail, a
woman said to me, 'What can I do for peace?'

I replied 'Let's see what the letters say.' The first one said, 'I'm a farm housewife. Since talking to you, I've realized I should be doing something for peace - especially since I'm raising four sons. Now I am writing one letter every day to someone in our government or in the United Nations who has done something for peace, commending them, to give them moral support.' The next one said, 'World peace seemed a bit too big for me, but since talking with you, I've joined the Human Relations Council in my town, and I'm working on peace among groups.' The third said 'Since talking with you I have resolved an unpeaceful situation between myself and my sister-in-law.' The last one said 'Since talking with you, I have cut out smoking.'

When a deep personal understanding is reached regarding approaches to peace in the world, we can discover the proper way of action according to our individual talents, abilities and interests.

However, when choosing a path of action, we must remember that all issues - whether personal or global - are interrelated. Since we as individuals lack both the time and energy to confront every issue, peace activists like Joanna Russ suggest that we focus primarily on those issues which affect us most directly, but to work with them in a manner which helps relate "our" issue to the larger problems facing humanity. For a student of ahimsa, the primary challenge is that human beings continue to choose the way of armed conflict to settle disputes. Unless we are willing to deal with this pattern on a fundamental level, the cycle of war and its preparation will continue to threaten our continued existence on this planet.

Chapter 5

Wealth Addiction, War and Ahimsa

How could we even begin to disarm greed and envy? Perhaps by being much less greedy and envious ourselves; perhaps by resisting the temptation of letting our luxuries become needs; and perhaps by even scrutinizing our needs to see if they cannot be simplified and reduced.

-E.F. Schumacher

ALTHOUGH MANY OF US SAY that we oppose war, we are often not aware of how the benefits we derive from our present economic system have contributed to poverty, unrest and war both here and in other parts of the world.

Our present standard of living - which requires large houses, plenty of food, nice bathrooms, home entertainment centers, spray deodorants, the latest smart phone and motor vehicles to the point of saturation - has become one of tremendous overconsumption. This is made possible by the unrestricted hoarding of limited food, minerals, energy and land, which often entails keeping them from the rest of the world. Although Western Europeans and North Americans make up only 15 per cent of the world's population, they consume well over 50 per cent of the world's resources.

Income inequality is believed to be one of the root causes of social unrest. Approximately half of the world's richest people (i.e. those with an annual income of $34,000 after tax) live in the United States (29 million), and fifteen million live in Western Europe. Others live primarily in Canada, Japan and Brazil. The Pew Research Center in Washington reported that in 2011, 71 percent of the global population was either classified as "poor" (living on $2 or less a day) or "low income" (living on between $2.01 and $10 a day).

The average income of just a quarter of the world's population is over $1,000 per capita, while more than half earn less than one-tenth this amount per year. This gap between the rich and the poor is one of the primary causes of political unrest in the world. For students of ahimsa, it is important to make the connection between the present opulent lifestyle of those living in the developed countries, and the poverty and suffering of the majority of those living in the developing nations of the world.

Because large companies understand the short-term economic advantages of purchasing food, manufacturing products and acquiring raw materials abroad, much of the wealth found in countries like the United States, Japan and Great Britain inevitably involves the exploitation of the people in developing nations, and does much to accentuate the repressive economic, political and social conditions which exist there.

In a country like Guatemala, for example, more than 75 percent of the people live below the poverty line. The wealthiest 10 percent own nearly 50 percent of the national wealth, while the poorest 10 percent own less than one percent of the national wealth. Two percent of landowners hold 65 percent of the arable land, and an estimated 78 percent of the farms use only 10 percent of the farmland. Some 38 percent of the working population— 1.8 million people—work in the declining agriculture sector. According to UNICEF, four in ten children (43.4 percent) under five are chronically malnourished; chronic malnutrition affects eight in ten (80 percent) indigenous Guatemalan children.

Like many developing nations, Guatemala has witnessed the strong presence of United States and European-based corporations, which have close ties to the nation's ruling elite. Together they have achieved virtual political and economic control of the country through long-term investment, and especially the purchase and/or control of the country's finest cropland. In Guatemala alone, for example, over one hundred large transnational companies are firmly rooted in the local economy, and are producing everything from cake mixes and milk to men's shirts, cement and animal feed. For the most part, the percentage of foreign ownership in these companies is approximately 70 percent, while the remaining 30 per cent is owned by the local ruling elite.

Such foreign operations of the top twenty-five American industrial corporations, for example, account for between 25 and 30 percent of total sales, assets and earnings. Because labor and related costs are lower than in the home country, the profits made from these operations have been estimated to be in excess of 20 per cent a year, and far outdistance profits made from domestic operations.

Trickle Down Economics

It has been argued, however, that much of the income of these multinational corporations "trickles down" to the local population, but this has not been found to be the case. During Brazil's famous economic boom of the 1960s and 1970s, when the gross national product increased by over 10 per cent each year, *The New York Times* reported that only 5 per cent of the estimated 100 million Brazilians benefited from five years of unprecedented growth, which was mostly channeled to the already rich members of the upper classes. Forty-five per cent actually saw their standard of living eroded during these years, and the rest lived as they had before the economic boom began.

As it is in the United States, the distribution of wealth is a major problem in Brazil. While Brazil's executives enjoy among the highest salaries in the world, the minimum salary was increased to R$622 (US$335) per month in 2012. According to the World Bank, in 2009, the poorest fifth of the Brazilian population received just 2.9 percent of the nation's income compared to 58.6 percent received by the richest fifth. Some thirteen million families, or 45 million people across Brazil, receive direct financial support from the *Bolsa Família* program. And between 2001 and 2011, *The Rio Times* reported that the population in Rio's *favelas* increased by 27.7 percent. In the same period, the rest of the city population grew by 3.4 percent, indicating a growing divide. The rates of violent crime remain among the highest in Latin America.

Some claim that foreign investment represents a boost to the national economy of the host nation and provides much-needed jobs which did not exist previously. While this may be true with entirely new industries, many modern enterprises are highly automated and only provide jobs for a small number of people. A modern dairy, for example, may employ less than half the number of workers of a traditional rural dairy to produce the same amount of milk.

In many cases, large, modern companies tend to compete with small locally owned enterprises (such as a grain mill, a dairy or a weaver's co-operative) and can force them out of business. Multinational companies rarely benefit the working people. Economic power and profits tend to be concentrated in the hands of the transnational itself and the local ruling elite, while contracts for agricultural products are often made with the landed aristocracy, the owners of the best cropland.

The Destruction of Indigenous Economies

In addition to extracting large quantities of minerals, inexpensively produced food and cheap manufactured goods for export, many multinationals are destroying the indigenous culture by "Europeanizing" or "Americanizing" it: flooding the market with expensive non-essential products that the people do not need. Soft drinks, fast food, canned fruits and vegetables, processed breakfast cereals, candy and other sweets, white flour products and cosmetics head the list. In many cases, the production of these goods wastes valuable resources which could be better devoted to producing traditional products of proven value. Cornflakes, for example, have widely replaced the nutritious and inexpensive corn tortilla in Mexico and Central America. As more people are led to believe that it is "old-fashioned" to consume tortillas for breakfast, competition for corn increases its price, thus making it more difficult to purchase.

In addition, much of the land which could be utilized to grow crops for domestic consumption is often devoted to growing crops for export. Our demand for "exotic" fruits like mangoes, pineapples, mandarin oranges and papayas has priced them out of the reach of the local people who have traditionally included them in their diet. In addition, the out-of-season demand for produce like strawberries, tomatoes and melons often utilizes valuable cropland which used to grow essential foods - like beans, corn and fresh vegetables - for the local population. Since labor costs are lower in Third World countries, these foods are much cheaper to produce than foods grown in the United States, Europe or Japan. In addition to bringing healthy profits to the agricultural transnational and its middlemen, farmers in the country receiving the imports suffer financially.

The misuse of cropland for export is especially prevalent with non-essential products like coffee, sugar and meat. By 2016, for example, India ranked as the number one exporter of beef in the world (nearly two million metric tons), while Nicaragua- one of the poorest countries in the Western Hemisphere- exported approximately 125,000 metric tons of beef, much of which was sold as fast-food hamburgers or made into pet food for American dogs and cats.

In order to preserve this favorable economic arrangement, the governments of the industrialized, well-off nations often support repressive and undemocratic governments that dominate the people living in the host country. The cycle of corruption, exploitation and repression helps to produce fertile ground for political unrest and violent revolution. When the threat of political unrest is finally made clear, the government of the richer country may send military hardware, advisors or even troops to protect the multinational's investment and help maintain the status quo. The poem *Thank You Tio Sam* by Mary Mackey speaks to the issue of United States exploitation in Latin America:

> We took their fish and left them bones
> took their copper and left them stones

took their fruit, took their oil,
took their lumber and stripped their soil,
made them grow coffee instead of com
so their children starved before they were
born
we took their cattle, took their meat
left their people with nothing to eat
built roads and ports to rob them faster
(Gringo aid is a national disaster)
and now we all wonder and brood
at Latin America's ingratitude.

Fair Trade

Removing all transnational corporations from foreign soil is both unrealistic and impractical. We live in a global economic village, where many essential products are imported and exported to preserve at least a minimum standard of living for everyone.

However, responsible governments in the developing nations should only welcome industry which will benefit all its citizens rather than just a few, and the executives and stockholders of multinational corporations should be aware of the overall impact their company can make on the host country rather than only concern themselves with short-term financial gain.

But more importantly, the wise choice of goods and services by consumers at home can help determine both the type and quality of imported products. For example, if consumers insist that the strawberries they buy be grown domestically, this choice could affect the use of land abroad. By insisting that the goods they purchase from a developing nation be made only by members of labor unions or worker co-operatives, they will be making a strong and positive statement towards right economics and will contribute - in their own small way - towards peace and equality in the exporting nation.

The growth of Fair Trade is very encouraging. Fair Trade is a global trade model and certification that allows shoppers to quickly identify products that were produced in an ethical manner. For consumers, Fair Trade offers a significant way to reduce poverty through their everyday shopping. For farmers and workers in developing countries, Fair Trade offers better prices, improved terms of trade, and provides them with the business skills necessary to produce high-quality products that can compete in the global marketplace.

Through Fair Trade, farmers and workers can improve their lives and plan for their futures. According to Fair Trade USA, by 2017 Fair Trade benefited more than 1.2 million farming families in 70 developing countries in Africa, Asia and Latin America. The most common products that are Fair Trade Certified ™ include coffee, tea and herbs, cocoa, fresh fruits and vegetables, sugar, beans and grains, flowers, nuts, oils and butters, honey and spices, wine and clothing.

In addition to buying Fair Trade Certified ™ products, consumers can influence corporations and government representatives by writing letters, making phone calls, participating in boycotts and by voting at stockholder meetings. Efforts can also be made to ensure that government bonds (as well as investments by banks and other private corporations) be invested in ways that will encourage the wise use of natural resources, promote justice and equality among workers, and help ensure fair working conditions. Individuals can also lobby corporations and governments asking them to avoid dealing with governments that practice racial segregation or oppression as part of their national policy.

Mahatma Gandhi wrote: "The extension of the law of non-violence in the domain of economics means nothing less than the introduction of moral values as a factor to be considered in international commerce." Until we use every available means to help reduce the gap between rich and poor, violence will continue to be the byword of the economic system.

Aparigrah: The Doctrine of Non-Possession

In the light of this problem, one of Gandhi's major interests was the doctrine of *aparigrah* or non-possession. It has also been translated as non-grasping or non-greediness. He felt that the accumulation of money and other property by the wealthy was always at the expense of the poor. In 1933 he wrote:

> Our ignorance or negligence of the Divine Law, which gives to man from day to day his daily bread and no more, has given rise to inequalities with all the miseries attendant upon them. The rich have a superfluous store of things which they do not need and which are, therefore, neglected and wasted, while millions are starved to death for want of sustenance.

Though written over eighty years ago, his message still is valid today. For the modern student of ahimsa, it is important to make the connection between our infinite personal demand for wealth and property in our own lives with the economic, social and economic conditions that affect poor people throughout the world. At the same time, we need to explore how our acquisition of material goods creates a vicious cycle of need, greed and possessiveness and how this affects us both individually and as a society.

Whether a person "owns" many possessions or few possessions is not the issue. From a point of view of ahimsa, there is nothing intrinsically wrong with having a home, buying a car, running one's own business, or enjoying nice clothes. There is nothing intrinsically wrong with earning money, going to the theater, or eating at a fine restaurant with family and friends.

The basic problem is that for many of us, our quest for more and varied possessions takes the form of an addiction to wealth rather than legitimate need for and enjoyment of material things. Clothing, shelter and food may be our three basic needs in life, but for many people, these basic needs are often distorted, and take on an exaggerated importance. We have food on our shelves when we are not hungry; we have clothes in our closets we never (or rarely) wear, and we invest heavily in appliances, electronic equipment, motor vehicles, furniture and other objects we really do not need and rarely use. Money is hoarded for the sake of making more money, and is not based on any concrete need.

The tendency to possess and control often stems from a feeling that we do not feel complete unless we have a full closet, a large refrigerator filled with food, a new car every two years, a health club membership, the latest audio or video system, and a larger and more expensive home. The desire to accumulate is closely linked with the need to hold on to possessions at all costs, even though we rarely, if ever, use them. Many people, for example, routinely hold on to clothing that is never worn, or insist on keeping an appliance in the kitchen that hasn't been used in years. Of course, society promotes the addiction to wealth through clever advertising, easy access to credit, and the idea that more is better. In fact, advertising has become so effective in encouraging wealth addiction that people often wander into stores looking for "something to buy" even though they already have everything they need.

Possessions: The True Cost

In many cases, the quest to accumulate more possessions involves tremendous energy. The preoccupation with monthly payments, ongoing maintenance, insurance, and security to protect what we have takes tremendous financial and emotional energy. The amount of work needed to pay for our possessions often prevents us from enjoying many of the pleasures in life which feed, support and gratify us on a deep personal level. In many cases, our possessions actually possess *us,* and reinforce feelings of fear, greed, stinginess, and the need to protect what we own at all costs.

The link between our personal addiction to wealth and all that it implies, and the political and economic policies on the national governmental level is very strong, and makes a definite impact on the state of the world as a whole. One's desire to keep people of other races out of one's neighborhood to protect property values is similar to a country limiting immigration to certain "desirable" ethnic groups. The desire to live beyond one's means through credit is parallel to the trend by governments to spend far beyond what they receive in taxes. My father once joked that if he modeled our family's finances on the financial policy of the government, he (and my mother) would probably be in prison.

Many have believed that materialism, which can be defined as "a value system that is preoccupied with possessions and the social image they project", is both socially destructive and self-destructive. It erodes both happiness and peace of mind and is associated with anxiety, depression and broken relationships. A series of three studies on the psychological impact of materialism was published in the psychological journal *Motivation and Emotion* [February 2014]. It showed that as people become more materialistic, their well being (including good relationships, autonomy and sense of purpose) diminishes. As they become less materialistic, it rises. The article read:

> Across all three studies, results supported the hypothesis that people's well-being improves as they place relatively less importance on materialistic goals and values, whereas orienting toward materialistic goals relatively more is associated with decreases in well-being over time. Study 2 additionally demonstrated that this association was mediated by changes in psychological need satisfaction. A fourth, experimental study showed that highly materialistic US adolescents who received an intervention that decreased materialism also experienced increases in self-esteem over the next several months, relative to a control group. Thus, well-being changes as people change their relative focus on materialistic goals.

After living a life of middle-class comfort, Peace Pilgrim gave away all of her possessions when she began her first pilgrimage for peace in 1953. Her only outward possessions were her dark blue tunic and canvas shoes. She also carried a comb, a pen and a small notepad. She only accepted food and shelter when offered, and was reported to be very resistant when offered items like new shoes to replace her worn canvas ones. Knowing that Peace Pilgrim wrote two letters that needed to be mailed, a friend offered her a book of stamps. Rather than accept the book of stamps, Peace Pilgrim told her that all she needed were two stamps. Speaking about possessions, Peace Pilgrim said:

> Unnecessary possessions are unnecessary burdens. If you have them, you have to take

care of them! There is great freedom in simplicity of living. It is those who have enough but not too much who are the happiest.

Wants and Needs

Living within one's means and enjoying a healthy relationship with money and material objects does not necessarily imply living a life of poverty, nor giving up what we really need. The actual object in question - be it a new suit, a smart phone or a watch - is also of little importance, since each object has a different meaning to different people. A complete set of expensive cooking utensils will have a different significance for someone who is a gourmet chef than for a person who simply wants to make a good impression on guests who visit the kitchen.

For the student of ahimsa, the larger issue involves truly understanding our relationship with material objects and what role - if any - they play in our lives aside from their functional or aesthetic purpose. To what extent does our ownership of the object affect our basic feelings of self-worth? Does it give us a sense of power or prestige? Does it add to our feelings of arrogance or self-importance? Does having the object increase our psychological dependency on it, or can we relinquish it easily? Is the possession fulfilling a genuine need in our life, or does it simply reinforce our dependency on appearance values? Is the possession taking us away from real fulfillment or personal enjoyment?

In many cases, the quest for possessions is a result of our not being grounded: not feeling at one with ourselves and the Earth, as discussed in Chapter 2. As we increase our dependency on "the outer" to achieve security and self-worth, we tend to become less grounded, and hence, more insecure. This may be one reason why people who accumulate money and possessions feel that they "never get enough" and often pursue wealth far beyond their genuine needs. It is interesting to compare the generosity of Earth-centered people like Native Americans with the hoarding of wealth so prevalent in modern industrial societies. In the book *The Sacred* the authors write:

> Giveaways were one method of distributing wealth among members of the community. They were also a way of acknowledging that the tribe was composed of related members, like a family, all of whom were dependent on each other. Giveaways demonstrated a person or family's wealth - they were always wealthy because they could afford to give away - they did not worry about the loss of their possessions they gave away because they knew they too would someday be the recipients of others' gifts . . . For in giveaways were symbolized one of the values basic to most Native American communities in aboriginal times: sharing and community responsibility towards its individual and kin members.

This belief was echoed more recently by Andy Albeita, the Governor of Isleta Pueblo in New Mexico:

> When the white man prays, he prays for what *he* wants for himself. When the Indian prays, he prays for other people. The last words of the Indian prayer are these: 'If there is anything left, let it be for me.' You do not hear the Anglos pray that way. This is our way. We shall keep it our way.

The generosity of Native Americans is in marked contrast to billionaires like Howard Hughes, H. L. Hunt, John D. Rockefeller and John Paul Getty, who accumulated more money and possessions than they could ever possibly use. The stinginess of these wealth addicts is legendary, and any charity they gave was mainly in the interest of public relations and government tax deductions. The trend of some modern billionaires to give away most their wealth to charitable endeavors while they are alive is a powerful contrast to those of times past.

Traditional religious holidays like Christmas and Hanukkah have become commercialized to the point that the acquisition of presents has become the most important part of the holidays. Americans spent over $1 trillion on holiday gifts in 2016, which was approximately $416 per adult. While this was good news for those who produced and sold these products, many people gave gifts that they couldn't afford and others received gifts that they didn't really need. In response, some organizations have begun to sponsor giveaways to those in need during the Holidays.

One example was Temple Sinai of Roslyn, New York, which sponsored an "Eight Nights of Giving" program to celebrate Hanukkah. Each day, members of the temple were asked to give their time or money to help members of the larger community. Activities included donating children's books to the New York City Department of Homeless Services Shelters, Lego sets to the Cancer Center for Kids at Winthrop University Hospital, money to support The American Foundation for Suicide Prevention and meals to help feed ten needy families in Nassau County, where the village of Roslyn is located.

Living Simpler

In a society in which wealth and material objects bring respect and status, possessions are highly sought after by both rich and poor. In response to this, some people have rejected material wealth entirely. Mahatma Gandhi was perhaps the foremost exponent of the doctrine of non-possession and suggested that everyone follow his lead: "Dispossessing myself of all property . . . has been a positive gain. I would like people to compete with me in my contentment. It is the richest treasure I own." His concept of voluntary poverty was embraced by many Christians, including members of the nonviolent Catholic Worker movement founded by Dorothy Day.

However, in many cases, those who eschew material wealth need to be aware of transferring their attachment towards nonmaterial things. Even though there are no finite boundaries to emotional, intellectual or spiritual pursuits, philosopher and teacher J. Krishnamurti addressed himself to their limitations in his third volume of *Commentaries of Living:*

> You may want to possess people, another may
> possess a whole series of ideas, while
> someone else may be satisfied with owning a
> few acres of land; but however much the
> objects may vary, all possession is essentially
> the same, and each will defend what he owns
> - or in the very yielding of it, will possess
> something else at another level.

There is no simple formula for freeing oneself from the attachment to possessions. The complicated mechanics of the desire to possess go very deep into the psyche and the solutions may involve much personal confrontation and the dispelling of illusions we may have cherished for years. Gandhi suggested that "The first thing is to cultivate the mental attitude that I will not have possessions or facilities denied to millions, and the next immediate thing is to rearrange our lives as fast as possible in accordance with that mentality."

For the student of ahimsa, perhaps the first step is to inquire courageously into the dynamics of possessiveness: how it manifests in our life, where are its roots, for what it may be a substitute, and what type of results does it produce for ourselves and for those around us. We also may want to explore the true price we pay by accumulating money and wealth for their own sake, and how our "closed hand" regarding money and possessions affects our family, our friends and the community as a whole.

On a practical level, one can experiment with living more simply. For one person, it might involve going through the wardrobe and donating whatever hasn't been worn during the previous year to charity. For another, it may involve giving away a treasured possession to someone who admires it. For others, it may involve relinquishing a relationship with another person, or giving up a cherished attitude or idea.

Some may want to simplify their lives on an economic level. They may refuse to take on new debts, cut up their credit cards or return them to the bank. For others, it may involve taking a cut in salary in order to enjoy an extra day or two with their families. It may involve the decision not to speculate on the stock market or buy investment property simply because it is the "thing to do". For others, it may lead them to sell their house and boat and move into a small cabin in the mountains. There may even be people who, in following the Native American tradition, have a give-away of their own, and donate their material possessions to people who are in need.

In some cases, these actions will produce initial feelings of fear or even dread, as we relinquish the possessions we have become attached to. However, by bravely confronting these fears, we can slowly begin to explore new and exciting territory within ourselves. Whatever we choose to do (or not to do) with our possessions, we begin to move towards a better, more grounded relationship with them. This will, in turn, lead to a more intelligent perspective on how we want to relate to material things, as well as to our friends, our family, and to the larger community around us.

As seen by the examples of Jesus Christ, the Buddha, Muhammad, St. Francis, Mother Theresa and others, the doctrine of non-possession was considered a major step towards both inner peace and peace among people. Peter Maurin, a co-founder of the Catholic Worker movement, spoke eloquently about the need to live simply in his poem *A Case for Utopia*:

> The world would be better off
> if people tried to become better,
> and people would become better
> if they stopped trying to become better off.
> But when everyone tries to become better,
> Everybody is better off.
> Everyone would be rich
> if nobody tried to become richer,
> and nobody would be poor if everybody tried
> to be the poorest.
> And everybody would be what he ought to be
> if everybody tried to be
> what he wants the other fellow to be.

The combination of living simply, non-possession and generosity towards those in need helps lay the foundations for a life grounded in ahimsa.

Chapter 6

The Nonviolent Warrior: The Soldier of Ahimsa

The practice of non-violence does not merely imply that the devotee himself shall follow the principle, but it goes further, inasmuch as no violence should be committed or condoned. And indifference is a virulent form of violence! Ahimsa, abstinence from any form of killing or harming, will help cultivate an attitude that will be very useful in eliminating warfare and maintaining world peace.

-Gurudev Chitrabhanuji

MUCH OF HUMANITY IS living in a revolutionary situation where institutionalized himsa is accepted as the normal state of affairs. For this reason, both the need for and the challenges facing an aspirant to a life of ahimsa are especially great at this point in human history, where the lives of all of the Earth's inhabitants are in danger of destruction.

Like the traditional army which calls its citizens to its ranks in time of war, the world needs a new kind of soldier - a soldier of ahimsa - to help save both humanity and the entire planet from extinction. Because our own lives and those of others are literally "on the line", the time for individual commitment, personal involvement, and dedication to goals has never been more appropriate than at this moment.

When we speak in terms of becoming "soldiers of ahimsa" or "spiritual warriors", we are of course not referring to making war on others. Chogyam Trungpa Rinpoche, the founder of the Naropa Institute and author of *Shambhala: The Sacred Path of the Warrior* spoke of the word "warrior" as being taken from the Tibetan word *pawo,* or "one who is brave."

When we speak of "spiritual" we are referring to the state of being that exists when we connect to what mystics have called the "unfathomable, omnipresent, unnamable, omniscient, intelligent and loving force" that stands behind and guides the evolution of manifestation in the universe. As a brave and compassionate individual whose goal is to serve the cause of peace through ahimsa, the spiritual warrior has a unique and highly important role as a leader, a teacher, a healer and a friend.

The Challenges at Hand

Although it is obvious that the world is confronted with a myriad of problems, the essential threats facing the planet can be divided into three basic areas, each creating many related issues and challenges of its own:

1. The threat of nuclear war. This threat is so serious that

public opinion polls reveal that most residents of the United States feel that a nuclear war will take place in their lifetimes, with the extinction of human civilization as a result.

2. This is closely followed by the fear of terrorism by religious extremists. After the attacks on the World Trade Center in New York City, the Pentagon in Washington, D.C. and the downing of United Airlines Flight 93 in Pennsylvania on September 11, 2001, the reality of global terrorism entered the mass consciousness of humanity, although terrorism existed long before that time.

3. The progressive destruction of the planetary ecosystem. This would include the threat of radioactivity from nuclear power plants and pollution from factories, toxic waste dumps, and car exhaust. It also encompasses the loss of valuable topsoil, the spreading of deserts, the destruction of the ozone layer, and marked changes in climate due to the heating up of the polar ice caps from pollution.

4. The increasing gap between the rich and the poor around the world and the misery and political tension it creates. Starvation, refugee migration, border conflicts between nations, terrorism, political unrest, corruption and crime are sources of urgent concern. The increased use of alcohol and especially drugs in both industrialized and developing countries are often linked to this vicious cycle of poverty and despair.

For the most part, these problems have been acknowledged (at least intellectually) by both individuals and government agencies, and various programs have been undertaken in an attempt to control them. However, since the efforts of both government agencies and private groups have been largely devoted to symptoms (such as providing food to refugees or adding more guards to police national borders), the root causes of these issues has not been dealt with effectively. For example, the wave of refugees who come to the United States from Central America can be traced to, in part, the U.S. government's support for corrupt local oligarchs who have suppressed democracy, brutalized their people and profited from drugs and gang violence. Similarly, the displacement of millions of refugees in the Middle East can often be traced to foreign governments that have exacerbated the underlying political and social problems that have existed there.

For an aspirant to a life of ahimsa, these seemingly overwhelming problems offer many valuable opportunities to help create lasting and palpable planetary change. Because ahimsa is grounded in the belief that there is a basic human wisdom that can help solve the world's problems, the soldier of ahimsa is asked to develop inner wisdom as well as compassion and bravery. And because ahimsa involves both reclaiming and mobilizing our personal power in the deepest sense, the soldier of ahimsa can be a potent agent for planetary transformation.

Ahimsa and Terrorism

Addressing the issue of terrorism in the light of ahimsa is not an easy task. Terrorism can be defined simply as "the use of violence and intimidation in the pursuit of political aims". While this would include state-sponsored terrorism like acts of war, most people fear terrorism by radical Islamic groups. Terrorist attacks -especially those involving suicide- are often seen as irrational acts that people who love and value life find difficult- if not impossible- to understand. The roots of terrorism are often deep and complex, and accepted ways to overcome terrorism often involve fighting violence with violence.

Many of us- the writer included- would welcome a clear and understandable blueprint that will eliminate terrorism through ahimsa. Yet the first steps involve seeking to better understand the roots of terrorism and explore creative ways to overcome it through nonviolent means.

The Roots of Terrorism

Mahatma Gandhi addressed his feelings towards terrorism in the journal *Young India* as far back as 1931:

> It is an unshakable faith with me that a cause
> suffers exactly to the extent that it is
> supported by violence. I say this in spite of
> appearances to the contrary. If I kill a man
> who obstructs me, I may experience a sense
> of false security. But this security will be
> short-lived. For I shall not have dealt with the
> root cause. In due course, other men will
> surely rise to obstruct me. My business,
> therefore, is not to kill the man or men who
> obstruct me, but to discover the cause that
> impels them to obstruct me, and deal with it.

So why do people adopt terrorism? Those who choose terrorism are trying to right what they perceive to be a social or political or historical wrong. They may have been stripped of their land or denied what they believe are their fundamental rights. Some adopt terrorism to protest what they see as injustice. This can be a corrupt political system, an economic system that they feel is stacked against them, or a justice system that they perceive as unfair. Many have linked religion- especially religious fundamentalism as well as a misunderstanding of religious precepts- as playing a role in terrorism as well. Finally, those who embrace terrorism believe that violence -or the threat of violence- will be effective in helping them achieve their goals. When people do not enjoy meaningful opportunities in their lives, and are alienated from the societies around them, and when they have grievances that go unaddressed, they are considered to be more at-risk for joining terrorist movements.

Exploring Nonviolent Solutions

Seeking to eliminate terrorism by military means alone doesn't work. Although some terrorists may be killed and their networks damaged or destroyed, many innocent people are often killed or injured as well. Using violence to stop violence leads to a cycle of violence, often leading people to adopt terrorism in the future.

Finding solutions to terrorism should be the work of every world citizen. Seeking to understand the differences in cultures, religions, beliefs and human behaviors is a major starting point. Advocating for peace, freedom and equality of all human beings- as opposed to one group of people- can help eliminate the roots of terrorism. We mentioned earlier how violence is regarded as normal in our society, and is widely promoted in movies, sports and toys. This calls for us to seek to "re-engineer" the minds of individuals by taking them away from a culture of violence and bringing them closer to a culture of peace.

Finally, terrorism is often based on ideology, and ideology cannot be destroyed through simple condemnation, let alone by military means. World citizens must develop an ideology of peace, but we also need to put this ideology into practice. According to Anne Cushman writing in *Yoga Journal*:

To be truly effective—indeed, to be a whole practice—our [spiritual] practice must inform the way we treat our friends and families, the products we buy, the politicians we vote for, the governmental policies we support and oppose, the beliefs we speak out for.

Creatively dealing with terrorism is not an easy task. It involves not only acknowledging the reality of terrorism, but also its causes. It calls on us to build a world where attentive and compassionate listening to the suffering endured by both sides in a conflict prevails over the escalation of violence. We also need to create a paradigm where the desire for genuine understanding overcomes our prejudices, our fears and our thirst for vengeance.

Another Type of Soldier

Unlike the traditional soldier who is a product of six to twelve months of regimentation and military discipline, the soldier of ahimsa develops as a result of years of deep inner exploration and self-confrontation. Instead of mindlessly following the orders of another, the soldier of ahimsa takes personal responsibility for every thought, word and action. In his book *Satyagraha,* the Indian scholar R. R. Diwakar spoke about the qualities of a soldier of ahimsa:

> The discipline for a nonviolent soldier is of a different kind. The one is to kill; the other to die. The one is to hate; the other to love. The one is to get angry; the other to remain patient. The one is to inspire fear; the other to overcome fear. The one is to inflict pain; the other to suffer pain without complaint.

As a result of this special orientation, all outward activities take on a different character and tone. Instead of causing fear, the soldier of ahimsa seeks to instill confidence and trust. In place of antagonism, the spiritual warrior works to bring about communication and understanding. As opposed to the defensiveness and bullying of the traditional soldier, the soldier of ahimsa is protected by humility and vulnerability. In place of contempt for the "enemy", the soldier of ahimsa offers goodwill and respect. Martin Luther King, Jr., wrote:

> The nonviolent resistor not only refuses to shoot his opponent but he also refuses to hate him. At the center of nonviolence is the principle of love . . . The nonviolent resistor would contend that in the struggle for human dignity, the oppressed people of the world must not succumb to the temptation of becoming bitter or indulging in hate campaigns. To retaliate in kind would do nothing but intensify the existence of hate in the universe. Along the way of life, someone must have sense enough and morality enough to cut off the chain of hate. This can only be done by projecting the ethic of love to the center of our lives.

The practice of ahimsa is grounded in truth, inner strength, and the courage to be compassionate, even in the face of danger. In many cases, the amount of courage to be compassionate is greater than the bravery needed to be violent, as the soldier of ahimsa confronts his or her own lower nature and seeks to transform its energy towards a higher and more creative level of manifestation.

A spiritual warrior is not passive, and does not necessarily repress anger or indignation. Jesus gave us a model of a soldier of ahimsa even when He overturned tables and threw the moneychangers out of the temple. His anger and righteous indignation were appropriate for the situation, and were free from the violence, injury and abuse which would normally accompany such a dramatic act. Like the Christ, the spiritual warrior must face up to and accept personal responsibility for the impact his or her thought and actions will have on others.

Is Killing Ever Justified?

In extreme cases, such as when a rabid dog or a berserk individual poses a direct threat to the safety of a child, there may be no alternative to prevent such a threat than through violent means when all other methods fail. Under these circumstances, a votary of ahimsa has the responsibility to act in the *least harmful manner* possible rather than to stand by and do nothing.

The motivation behind the action in any situation must be acknowledged to see whether the act is grounded in compassion or is the result of anger or fear. His Holiness Tenzin Gyatso, the 14th Dalai Lama, addressed this issue during the Centenary Convention of the Theosophical Society in 1975:

> I believe that having a sympathetic heart, a warm heart, a kind heart, is the essence or the most important thing. Irrespective of whether you believe in a religion or not, or no matter what ideology you follow, if you have this . . . then even such a violent act of killing someone, if it is done with a really good motive, could go beyond the usual level of killing.

In essence, the motivation behind any action determines the degree of ahimsa often more than the outward act itself.

Those who have advocated ahimsa are well aware that at our particular stage of human evolution, self-defense is often a necessary part of national policy and that war among groups is often a fact of life. For many of us, brave women and men who serve in the country's armed forces defend us and also fight in our name, often at tremendous personal cost. For this reason, they and their families deserve our respect, support and gratitude for their sacrifice, even if we are philosophically against militarism and war.

Ahimsa and War

Teachings regarding ahimsa in times of war go back many centuries, and have been updated to meet modern-day needs. One of the primary precepts of ahimsa teaches that war should be avoided through sincere and truthful dialogue. It also teaches that:

-Force must be the last resort.

-If war becomes necessary, its cause must be just, its purpose must be virtuous, and its objective must be to restrain the wicked through lawful means.

-The ultimate goal of war must be peace.

weapons used in war must be proportionate to the ~d the aim of war, rather than indiscriminate on.

-All strategies and weapons used in the war must be to defeat the opponent, but not to cause them unnecessary misery, such as the use of cluster bombs or napalm.

-Warriors must use their judgment in the battlefield.

- Cruelty towards the opponent during war is forbidden.

-Wounded or unarmed opponents must not be attacked or killed, and those who are wounded must be given medical treatment.

-Special care must be taken to assure that children, women and civilians not be injured.

-While war is in progress, sincere dialogue for peace must continue.

Self-Defense

Self defense is also permitted by ahimsa, because some people will- whether out of ignorance, error, hatred or fear- attack others. According to Morihei Ueshiba, the founder of the nonviolent martial art of Aikido, the goals of ahimsa must be to neutralize the aggression of the attacker and avoid conflict as much as possible.

He taught that the best defense is one where the victim is protected, as well as where the attacker is respected and not injured whenever possible. Under both ahimsa and Aikido, there are no enemies, and appropriate methods of self-defense focus on neutralizing the immaturity, assumptions and aggressive strivings of the attacker.

In Japan, this practice extends to modern law enforcement. Japan has one of the lowest rates of violent crime in the world, especially involving guns, which are extremely difficult to obtain. Although many police carry guns in Japan, they are discouraged from using them: they focus instead on attaining a high degree of skill in traditional martial arts instead. According to a report by BBC news, "The response to violence is never violence, it's always to de-escalate it. Only six shots were fired by Japanese police nationwide [in 2015]. What most Japanese police will do is get huge futons and essentially roll up a person who is being violent or drunk into a little burrito and carry them back to the station to calm them down."

Ahimsa is never passive, but involves dynamism and clarity. Mahatma Gandhi was very forceful when he taught that ahimsa goes beyond what is traditionally called "window dressing". When nonviolence is used as a gesture or as a mask to hide a seething violence within, he felt that it could be more pernicious than a violent act which is honest and direct. Gandhi once said that when nonviolence is used to mask fear or impotence, it is far better to be violent. He added that there is some hope for the violent, but rarely any hope for the impotent.

Focusing on the Causes

Finally, a traditional soldier is trained to respond largely to situations that are symptomatic of deeper problems, while the spiritual warrior actively seeks to deal with the underlying causes of violence and strife. While an outer situation can serve as a focus and a catalyst for action, the deeper task involves going beyond the appearances of an issue and contacting the underlying distortions, misunderstandings or fears which motivate the destructive attitude or violent act.

Such a task requires tremendous courage and involves a deep and compassionate understanding of oneself and others. By dealing with the essence of the problem rather than merely the symptom, one can bring about a lasting transformation rather than a mere pseudo-solution.

The central task for a soldier of ahimsa is to be able to "feel with" another: to respond to the challenge of the moment with caring, warmth and compassion. This is not to say that a spiritual warrior is governed only by feelings, and does not allow the guidance of common sense dictated by the rational mind. However, unlike the traditional soldier who is ruled chiefly by the mind and rigid authoritarian structures, the soldier of ahimsa responds primarily to heart feelings, which in turn work with the concrete and abstract mind, the intuition, and the power of positive will.

Overcoming Emotional Paralysis

For most of us, the threat of nuclear war, the loss of our planetary life-support systems through pollution, the threat of terrorism, and the suffering and grief in the world are nothing short of emotionally overwhelming.

When confronted with the reality of our homes, family and friends being decimated by a nuclear blast, we often "cut off" emotionally from our feelings of fear, grief, anger, guilt as well as the frustration brought about by our feelings of helplessness. When we see a homeless person on the street trying to find warmth in a doorway, we often look the other way, hoping to avoid the feelings of pain and guilt that come up. When we hear about widespread corruption in city government, we often throw up our hands and say "Politicians! What else can you expect?" and continue watching the football game. When we read that increased amounts of money have just been allocated to expand our nuclear arsenal while our neighbors cannot afford health care, part of us simply does not want to know about it.

As a result of suppressing these genuine feelings (which we are taught to contain since earliest childhood) we often place ourselves in a state of paralysis and powerlessness. We are overwhelmed by the pervasive feeling that the world is going to ruin and there is little, if anything, we can do to save it.

The need to overcome the obstacle of emotional paralysis is one of the spiritual warrior's greatest tasks because our emotions contain the seeds of positive action. The word itself comes from the latin *e*, "out" and *movere*, "to move." Emotions - when properly channeled - provide us with both the energy and the passion needed to find creative solutions to our problems and express them through concrete deeds.

Years ago before graduating from college, I visited a slaughterhouse in Madison, Wisconsin, on a dare. After being taken on an extensive tour of the kill floor where I witnessed the slaughter of over a thousand pigs and cows, I was filled with feelings of anger and grief. Though already a vegetarian, the tour of the slaughterhouse was a revelation. I experienced nightmares for weeks, and often "smelled" the slaughterhouse while attending classes or studying for exams. These feelings also included those of irrational violence, including blowing up the slaughterhouse with bombs.

My emotional reactions to the slaughterhouse experience became the catalyst for my first book, *Eating for Life: A Book about Vegetarianism,* first published by Quest Books (an imprint of the Theosophical Publishing House) in 1972. Although I wasn't fond of library research and documentation during my high school and college years, the book contained several hundred scientific and historical references, charts, diagrams and notes. Whenever I became bored or tired with the project, I would think back to the visit to the slaughterhouse and return to work. The emotional trauma of seeing the animals killed was the catalyst which brought the work to completion. The book was ready for the publisher after six months, while I was holding down a full-time job.

There are several basic steps required to break out of the paralysis brought about by anger and grief. The first step is to acknowledge our feelings, especially those of pain, grief, anger and fear. This can take the form of writing down our thoughts in a private journal, to speak out in active prayer, or in sharing our feelings with a close friend or relative. Some individuals have formed support groups where feelings of fear, despair and anger are shared in a supportive and nurturing space. Some groups incorporate the use of rubber bats and pillows to facilitate the full (and often irrational) expression of these pent-up emotions - which may include hatred and cruelty - safely and dynamically.

Acknowledge the Negative, Uncover the Positive

It is also important to acknowledge even the most negative of our emotions, not only because they are indeed a part of us, but if not expressed, they can cause harm. Internalized rage, for example, can later manifest in health problems, or can express itself outwardly in covert himsa towards family, friends or co-workers.

At the same time, emotions we view as negative often can serve as a "cover" for more positive qualities, which are often repressed as well. For example, violence contains the seeds of positive assertion, while anger often covers up feelings of righteous indignation and the desire for justice. Guilt related to the acknowledgement of these repressed human emotions constricts us on physical, emotional and mental levels, and we become paralyzed and "stuck" as a result. According to peace activist and feminist Barbara Deming, our goal, then, is to "transmute the anger

99

that is often affliction into the anger that is determination to bring about change".

By exploring these emotions with commitment, love and even humor, we can begin to free ourselves from their grasp. By laying them out before us for examination and understanding, we begin to assume control over the role they have played in our lives. By doing so, we begin to reclaim the positive "core qualities" that these negative emotions represent. Competition can be transformed into the desire to do one's best for its own sake, while anger can be transformed into concrete acts of service to others. The resulting passion, wisdom and energy will enable us to discover new and creative ways of dealing with the issues facing us and the rest of humanity, and will help us change the world.

The Art of Identification

Another aspect of this work is to strive to identify ourselves with a political or social problem by coming into close emotional contact with it. A unique concept towards integrating personal and political reality was developed by members of the Political Science Committee at the Pathwork Center in New York. Their process utilized role-playing, group interaction, simulation, and other methods to uncover the specific dynamics of a political or social issue.

> Political struggles, regardless of how complex
> or unique they appear, are manifestations of
> our personal spiritual struggles. We therefore
> approach each issue by first experiencing our
> relationships to it. How does the outer
> conflict reflect an inner conflict that we
> share? In what ways are the forces blocking
> resolution a reflection of our own resistance

to resolution? What are the operant unconscious motivations that needlessly prolong the conflict? How can these conflicts be resolved on the level of the personality and what do the solutions tell us about resolving political struggles?

Through this process of identification, we can learn to see the problems facing humanity on more personal, intimate terms. At the same time, we can also see our role in both the creation of these problems and in their resolution. In exploring such sensitive areas, observe how the negative aspects of institutions (such as government, schools or business) often mirror the negative aspects found in many of us. As an example, we can look at a bank that willingly lends money to a dictatorial regime and relate that to how we relinquish our ethical values to obtain what we want. Like the corrupt politician, do we ever manipulate others to obtain their recognition or support? Consider the preacher who threatens his congregation with hellfire and brimstone and equate that with how we use fear and guilt in order to gain control over others.

Such critical self-examination is often a difficult process, because most of us would rather not be identified with the traits we see as destructive. Some people particularly are resistant to this self-examination because they believe that greed, violence and corruption cannot be transformed on either personal or institutional levels. Curiously enough, those who have sought to look at these traits objectively have discovered that they do not occupy their entire beings, and when they are exposed, owned up to and worked with, actually begin to lose their power.

By exploring these deeper levels within ourselves, we can more closely identify with others, and can more personally feel their pain, conflicts, hopes and fears. By removing the barriers between "us" and "them" we can better understand the plight of the homeless, the frustrations of the unemployed, the worldview of the religious extremist, the paranoia of the military officer, and the corruption of the business executive, educator or politician.

In addition, actively learning about the lives of other people helps us to more closely identify with them. By finding out more about another person's ethnic group or religion (and perhaps attending their religious services) we can learn to understand and appreciate their beliefs, traditions and customs.

Many of us love to travel, and individual or group travel as a "planetary goodwill ambassador" is important. By learning at least some of the country's language, history and traditions before we leave, we can come into greater contact with the local residents, and open ourselves to their friendship and way of life. Some organizations offer trips and citizen exchanges to facilitate meeting people in other countries.

When we travel with awareness and consciousness, personal travel and citizen exchanges (as well as performing volunteer work in another country) can do much to help break down barriers among people of different nations and can form the foundation for planetary peace at a grassroots level. While each of us will probably continue to embrace our own cultural, political or religious convictions, we will learn to "cherish the differences" and relate to others with greater understanding and respect.

When we closely identify with others, we cease to regard them as faceless enemies. Rather, they are considered individual human beings with similar struggles, failings and aspirations to our own. Though we may have serious differences, we begin, as Gandhi said, to "hate the sin and not the sinner". We can then begin to work to resolve these difficulties from a point of *collaboration* rather than through a protracted struggle between adversaries.

This new understanding can bring about a myriad of creative opportunities for a spiritual warrior. Whatever one's path, the soldier of ahimsa must be aware of the underlying motives which lead to outer action and take responsibility for even the most subtle aspects of the personality which influence all thoughts and actions. Despite the challenge, a spiritual warrior can be a disciplined, clear-thinking, and compassionate agent for change in the world. Such a task is indeed a challenge, yet it is not for the few. Mahatma Gandhi wrote:

> My optimism rests on my belief in the infinite possibilities of the individual to develop nonviolence. The more you develop it in your own being, the more it overwhelms your surroundings and by and by might oversweep the world.

"Growing Corn"

Many years ago, I attended a workshop conducted by the Native American teacher and healer Sun Bear, who was best known for his Medicine Wheel Gatherings during the 1980s and 1990s. Although Sun Bear's primary message to us that day was to live in harmony with Nature, I remember the following statement: "I don't care much about a person's philosophy unless it can grow corn."

For a soldier of ahimsa, a major goal is to discover where our energies and talents should be channeled in a practical way. Although a basic shift in consciousness is essential for ahimsic work, feelings of compassion, peace and brotherhood are of little value unless they are expressed in practical day-to-day reality. In addition to a conceptual grounding in the philosophy of ahimsa, we require specific tools and tactics to help maximize our efforts.

Training in nonviolent persuasion and protest is useful for a soldier of ahimsa to achieve both efficiency and effectiveness towards bringing about change in the world. These avenues include nonviolent communication through public speaking, debates, letters, declarations and petitions. They may involve learning how to work effectively with the media, and in creating press releases, graphics, leaflets, banners and the staging of media events.

For those with organizing skills, learning how to stage events like public assemblies, parades, marches, teach-ins, mock funerals and pilgrimages is useful. Being trained in the teachings of nonviolent disciplines, methods to increase self-esteem and fearlessness, and strategies in how to alter power relationships among groups are especially recommended for those who are drawn to civil disobedience and non-cooperation.

And while such public activism is important, we need to visualize the long term goals of our effort. Many people, for example, may go to a demonstration and return home feeling "mission accomplished". Yet their efforts may be only a first step in a larger plan, which may require open-mindedness and flexibility. Duncan Green, Head of Research at Oxfam Great Britain and author of *How Change Happens*, offered the following advice to political activists during a National Public Radio interview in early 2017:

> You have to be an activist and a 'reflectivist'
> at the same time. That's someone who
> reflects on the systems evolving, how these
> institutions are structured. You have to
> understand the system to know who might be
> your ally. And there has to be a little part of
> you that acknowledges doubt, ambiguity and

uncertainty. You have to have room to change direction.

Others soldiers of ahimsa may seek to learn nonviolent martial arts such as Aikido, which espouses the *aiki* concept of harmonizing oneself with an attacker. Many of these teachings are discussed in books like *The Dynamics of Nonviolent Action* (Part 3 of the series *The Politics of Nonviolent Action)*, by Gene Sharp, and information on nonviolent training and tactics is available through groups like the War Resistors International, the American Friends Service Committee, and the Fellowship for Reconciliation listed in the Appendix.

The specific opportunities for a soldier of ahimsa are both numerous and varied. They can encompass working for inner peace, peace among individuals, and peace among groups and nations. The following is but a partial list of suggestions for the concrete expression of ahimsa in the world, some of which offer exciting and creative possibilities for each person reading this book.

Individual "One to One"

-Adopt personal habits regarding diet, clothing, entertainment and employment that are nonviolent and life-affirming.

-Live a life grounded in honesty, truthfulness, generosity and compassion

-Resolve specific conflicts in relationships with others.

-Communicate peace by writing letters to newspapers, elected representatives, non-elected representatives (United Nations delegates, heads of companies, schools, foreign diplomats, etc.). A phone call or "snail mail" letter gets more attention than an e-mail, or your name on a petition.

-Contact radio and television call-in shows to express your views.

-Become a citizen diplomat. Make personal contact with those you meet on your international travels.

-Boycott companies that exploit their workers or which do not serve the cause of peace; accompany the boycott with a letter to the company explaining your action.

-Withhold taxes destined for military purposes.

-Speak out about peace to neighbors, co-workers and to local groups.

-Become a "peace resource person" in your neighborhood or community. Distribute books and pamphlets on peace to libraries, schools and individuals.

Ahimsa out in the world: possibilities for group action

Join or start a group which works in the areas of:

-Feeding the hungry
-Sheltering the homeless
-Promoting nuclear disarmament
-Helping victims of domestic violence
-Drug education and prevention
-Preserving the environment
-Working to end sex-trafficking
-Saving whales and dolphins
-Promoting vegetarianism

-Campaigning for animal rights
-Fighting for gun control
-Community clean-up and rehabilitation
-Protecting the rights of the physically or mentally handicapped
-Ending nuclear energy and nuclear waste dumps
-Peace meditation
-War tax resistance
-Hospices for the sick
-Nonviolent national defense

Every Act is Important

Shortly before he left office, President Barack Obama reflected that the role of each individual in helping improve the world situation during an interview published in *The New Yorker* magazine. He believed that this role must combine both inner reflection and concrete action, as well as determination to never give up:

> And your job as a citizen and as a decent
> human being is to constantly affirm and lift
> up and fight for treating people with kindness
> and respect and understanding. And you
> should anticipate that at any given moment
> there's going to be flare-ups of bigotry that
> you may have to confront, or may be inside
> you and you have to vanquish. And it doesn't
> stop... You don't get into a fetal position
> about it. You don't start worrying about
> apocalypse. You say, O.K., where are the
> places where I can push to keep it moving
> forward.

No matter how difficult the situation, we must remember that every act of ahimsa - however small and insignificant it may appear - is adding to the total peace picture. By becoming aware of our individual talents, as well as the needs of the community, we can begin to channel our efforts into one or more concrete areas of service. According to Peace Pilgrim:

> When you do something for world peace,
> peace among groups, peace among
> individuals, or your own inner peace, you
> improve the total peace picture. Whenever
> you bring harmony into any unpeaceful
> situation, you contribute to the cause of
> peace.

As spiritual warriors from all nations, religions and cultures unite towards integrating the essence of ahimsa into their everyday lives, a planetary transformation of consciousness can take place. This will gradually yet forcefully transform the institutions of society, so that they will begin to serve the cause of peace in the world and preserve our planetary home for the benefit of all of its inhabitants.

Part III

Ahimsa and Other Animals

ALTHOUGH HUMAN BEINGS EAT other animals for food, perform laboratory experiments on them, hunt them for sport, trap them for their fur and use them for entertainment, we rarely pause to consider whether our practices are ethically defensible.

Although perceptions have changed over the past twenty years or so, many people greet the concept of animal rights with sarcasm and derision. Those who champion the welfare of other animals are often regarded as sentimental bleeding hearts or outright crackpots. Since most of us have been taught the Biblical perspective that "man has dominion over the animals", the idea that species other than our own should have rights sounds absurd.

Nevertheless, a growing number of people have been viewing the plight of other animals with deep concern. Although humans may have needed to kill members of other species in the past, many feel that the "kill-or-be-killed" philosophy of survival is not only antiquated but dangerous. In today's world, the fate of one species in an ecosystem can eventually have an impact on the fate of all the others. As more and more species are being decimated by human populations or radically increased in numbers by unnatural means, the long-term welfare of humanity itself is being brought into serious question.

Those who promote animal rights take the position that although other animals cannot reason or speak as humans do, this does not give us the right to do with them as we like. Even though our possession of a soul and superior intelligence are used to create an arbitrary dividing line over rights, the fact remains that all animals have the capacity to experience pain and suffering, and in suffering they are our equals.

Most people do not realize the magnitude of the plight of the other animal species. Certain events, such as the slaughter of whales and baby seals, have begun to elicit concern and concrete action. When details of a United

States Department of Defense Proposal to use 200 beagles to test poisonous gases became public in 1973, the Department received more letters in protest that it had received about the bombing of North Vietnam.

Though human concern for other animals is primarily limited towards those animals which elicit positive feelings like dolphins, pedigree puppies and baby seals, more people are becoming aware of the total picture of animal suffering. During the past few years a wide variety of animal rights organizations have been established, and many older groups have become more active and broadly based. Some of the more progressive groups have sponsored consciousness-raising workshops designed to help people de-condition themselves of stereotyped attitudes regarding other animals. Terms like "human chauvinism" and "speciesism" (defined by philosopher Peter Singer as a prejudice or attitude of bias towards the interests of one's own species and against those of members of another species) have become part of our vocabulary. Some excellent books, such as Dr. Singer's *Animal Liberation,* have been written to educate the public about many of the aspects of animal suffering and exploitation, and have received wide attention.

During the 1960s, world concern was focused primarily on abolishing war among people, and while these efforts continue, later decades reflected a growing interest in halting war against the environment. As a logical extension of this new ecological awareness, the concern about endangered animals has brought the largely unrecognized "inter-species war" between human beings and other animals into sharp focus.

The concept of an inter-species war is not a new one. Dr. George S. Arundale, the third President of the Theosophical Society, shared his larger view when asked his opinion of the prospects of the League of Nations in 1926.

A league to abolish war between the human
and animal kingdoms, an inter-kingdom war,
is far more important than a league to abolish
inter-human war. The latter, at least, is more
or less a war among equals, among those who
can, more or less, fight back. There may be
some honor, some dignity, some self-respect,
in such a war. But war in which one side is
practically omnipotent and the other side
practically impotent is no war at all, it is just
massacre, just the pitting of mental cunning
against weak ignorance.

Since the unity and interdependence of all life is
now recognized as a fact of nature, there has been deep
concern about the long term effects of an inter-species war,
not just for the animals which are the immediate victims,
but for the long-term survival of the human species as well.

Ahimsa may be radical, but it is not fanatic. The
primary goal of ahimsa is to eliminate all injury to other
life forms, not just because it is best for our conscience,
well-being and future, but because it is every animal's
earthly right to enjoy a life free of slavery, injury, suffering
and premature death at the hands of the more powerful
human species.

The following chapters will explore some of the
areas of concern to a student of ahimsa: the use of animals
for food and experimentation, using animals for
entertainment and recreation, animals as servile products,
the ownership of animals and other fundamental issues of
related importance.

Some of the information presented in these sections
will stir up strong emotions, and may make you angry or
sad. Nevertheless, please examine these often controversial
issues with an open mind and heart. Understanding our

relationship with other animals is - at this critical period in our history – an essential part in making ahimsa a living reality in the world.

Chapter 7

Animals for Food

Personally, I have decided that I do not want to kill.
I see a sheep in the field - let it live;
I see a cow in the field - let it live;
I see some other creature - let it live;
I do not want to kill for me.

-John B.S. Coats

THE PRACTICE OF EATING ANIMALS for food appears to extend as far back as the Ice Age, when, anthropologists say, early Homo sapiens abandoned a plant-orientated diet in favor of one containing meat. The custom of meat-eating has continued to the present day, whether through necessity (as with the Inuit of Northern Canada) or through habit, conditioning or lack of knowledge, as is the case with most meat-eaters today.

The killing of animals for their meat has been a subject of great concern for proponents of ahimsa since the times of Lord Mahavira, the founder of the Jain religion, over 2,500 years ago. Modern advocates maintain that meat is not necessary for human survival, and that its production involves a long and cruel process of forced imprisonment, biological manipulation, transportation over long distances in crowded conditions, and finally a violent death on a slaughterhouse kill floor.

Meat-packing is a major business in the Western industrialized nations. In the United States alone, the production of meat involves over $225 billion in yearly sales, making the meat purveyors the largest segment of the nation's food industry. The meat business is also gaining in importance in the developing nations of the world, some of which devote a large percentage of their resources to raising animals to be slaughtered for export.

By 2016, an average person living in the United States or Canada consumed approximately 105 kilograms (232 pounds) of meat a year. An individual living in Great Britain or Northern Europe ate approximately 40 per cent less, while an Australian or New Zealander consumed approximately 20 per cent more. In order to satisfy the demand for meat in the United States alone, some 279,534,000 cattle, 1,077,369,000 hogs, 20,366,000 sheep and lambs, 8, 186,546,000 chickens, 224, 361,000 turkeys, and 24,742,000 ducks were slaughtered during the eleven months between January and November 2016. During a 70-year lifetime, the meat demanded by the average American involves the slaughter of approximately 11 adult cattle, 1 calf, 3 lambs and sheep, 23 pigs, 45 turkeys, 1,100 chickens and some 862 pounds (392 kilograms) of fish.

Over the years, reformists have worked to reduce the amount of violence involved in the slaughter of livestock for food. The most important result of their efforts has been the passage of laws which ensure that animals used for food are rendered unconscious at the moment of slaughter. Although it is gratifying to see that many of these "humane slaughter" statutes are on the books, much needs to be done to guarantee their strict enforcement, and to extend these regulations to the slaughter of birds, which are often killed without prior stunning.

Although many humanitarians have concentrated their energies towards the pre-slaughter treatment of livestock at the abattoir, the welfare of animals used in food production involves much more.

The Factory Farm

Although some people maintain that even the traditional methods of keeping and raising livestock animals involve a certain degree of exploitation, human beings have never in the past exploited them so ruthlessly as we do today.

Since the early 1950s, the increased demand for animals and their products has caused farming to evolve into a highly centralized and competitive business, with the sole objective being to obtain the highest possible ratio of output (such as meat, eggs and milk) to input (including shelter, fodder, water, medicine, equipment and labor costs).

Over the past few decades most of the animals involved in food production in the industrialized countries have been raised by inhumane "battery" methods, which have turned the pastoral farm of yesterday into an efficient and mechanized animal factory.

Many creatures - especially pigs, chickens and calves - never see the light of day until they are taken to the slaughterhouse. Calves are routinely taken from their mothers before they are a day old and live from six to eight weeks, chained in small wooden crates, until they are butchered for veal. Dairy cows are kept as long as they are good milk producers, after which they are killed for meat.

Chickens are perhaps most cruelly treated of all animals used for food. Often kept in windowless climate-controlled sheds, they spend their 8-9-week lives in extremely cramped and stress- producing conditions, with often four birds squeezed into one 18" X 24" cage. According to Peter Singer's landmark book *Animal Liberation:*

> Feather-pecking and cannibalism have
> increased to a formidable extent of late years,
> due, no doubt to . . . boredom, overcrowding
> in badly ventilated houses . . . lack of feeding
> space, unbalanced food or shortage of water,
> and heavy infestation of insect pests.

Genetic engineering has also played a major role in farm animal production, especially involving chickens. According to the British organization Compassion in World Farming:

> Today's conventional chickens have been
> selectively bred to grow so big, so fast they
> often cannot support the weight of their own
> unnaturally large breasts. This fast growth
> can have other dire consequences for the
> birds, such as leg deformities, heart attacks,
> footpad dermatitis, hockburns, and more. On
> top of that, the birds are kept in overcrowded
> houses with no access to natural light or the
> outdoors, and denied enrichment that
> encourages natural behavior.

Many animal rights campaigners have worked towards more compassionate treatment of these animals, and have urged the enactment of laws to guarantee more humane conditions for all livestock animals during their

117

lifetime. Perhaps the most active groups in the United States is the Farm Animal Rights Movement. Among its many activities, it sponsors an annual *Meatout,* World Day for Farmed Animals and Compassionate Holidays. Compassion in World Farming proposed the following requirements for intensive animal farming applicable to all animals raised for food and clothing:

1. *Movement:* Freedom from permanent tethering, stalling and caging. Livestock should be able to turn round, stand up and lie down on either side without difficulty, and to extend the head and all limbs fully in any natural direction whether standing or lying down.

2. *Exercise:* The ability to exercise daily by the natural methods of activity.

3. *Rest:* Access to a clean bedded area for housed stock or to clean pasture for stock on range.

4. *Water:* Access to clean water at all times of the day from the age of three weeks or earlier according to species and climate.

5. *Food:* Adequate, regular and palatable food suitable for the particular age and species - without added drugs or chemicals except as prescribed by a veterinary surgeon. Roughage for ruminants over two weeks of age.

6. *Environment:* Suitable environmental conditions to include shelter from extremes of weather if on range. Temperature, ventilation, and humidity to be maintained within certain maxima and minima wherever in controlled environment housing.

7. *Light:* Adequate lighting throughout the hours of daylight. Daylight to take precedence over artificial lighting. Window area to be between one-tenth and one-fifteenth of the total floor area.

8. *Mutilation:* Freedom from mutilations as far as possible. Mutilation only to be carried out by a veterinary surgeon. This mandate to include castration.

9.   *Transport:* Not to be transported for purposes of sale more than once in any period of eight weeks. Not to be transported for slaughter more than 60 miles.

10.   *Slaughter:* To be carried out only by the most painless method possible.

Governments have often refused to implement these recommendations on the grounds that they are not practical, although many individual farmers have, knowing that healthy animals that are treated well often produce a better product that can be sold at higher prices. For example, a growing number of egg producers, for example, have begun selling "free range" and "cage free" eggs. Although "organic" does not necessarily mean cage-free, the National Organic Program- which many organic egg producers subscribe to- requires that the poultry receive organic feed, are allowed to live cage-free, and have "outdoor access." There isn't, however, any mandate about how much time the chickens need to spend outdoors.

Towards Eliminating Animal Cruelty

There are probably many people who feel that factory farming and animal slaughter involve an unjustifiable degree of exploitation of sentient creatures, and yet believe that there is nothing wrong with rearing and killing animals for food provided that it is done humanely.

This view is strongly contested by many people in the animal rights movement, who say that as long as we think that an animal may be killed simply so that we can satisfy our taste for meat, we are still victims of the human chauvinist point of view that views species other than our own as mere objects to be used and manipulated for our pleasure. They add that if we were to raise animals so that they lived and died without suffering, we would discover that to achieve this goal at present production levels would be impossible. Meat and other animal products would be so expensive that only the very rich could afford them.

There are a number of courses of action one can take towards eliminating cruelty to animals used for meat. One can write letters to legislators, newspapers and companies involved in meat production in support of humane animal treatment. One can also boycott specific products made by companies which systematically abuse animals. However, the most effective method is to help eliminate the demand for animal foods and thus cease to contribute to the type of industry that profits from the exploitation and suffering of livestock animals.

Becoming a vegetarian is the most effective way to accomplish these goals, since a personal boycott of meat is a direct and concrete statement regarding one's commitment to eliminate cruelty to animals used for food. For many humanitarians, this step can be a difficult one, as talk ends and action begins. In his book *Animal Liberation,* Peter Singer addresses this problem directly:

> It is easy to take a stand about a remote issue, but the speciesist, like the racist, reveals his true nature when the issue comes nearer home. To protest about bull-fighting in Spain or the slaughter of baby seals in Canada while continuing to eat chickens that have spent their lives crammed into cages, or veal from calves that have been deprived of their mothers, their proper diet, and the freedom to lie down with their legs extended, is like denouncing apartheid in South Africa while asking your neighbors not to sell their houses to blacks.

The adoption of a plant-based diet is not nearly as much of a sacrifice as many people believe. During the past few decades, plant-based diets have gained tremendous popularity around the world, and many well-known public figures, including actors, writers, political leaders and professional athletes, have found that a diet without meat provides every element necessary for a dynamic, creative and healthy life.

Types of Vegetarians

There are several kinds of vegetarian diets, but they all have one thing in common: no animal flesh, be it from a cow, pig, sheep, bird or fish.

Lacto-ovo vegetarians: People who abstain from meat are known as lacto-ovo vegetarians. In addition to plant foods, milk, cheese and eggs play an important role in their diet. The primary ethical rationale behind the lacto-ovo-vegetarian diet is that the production of eggs and milk involves the natural body processes of the animal and that the cow or hen is not killed in order for humans to obtain their products. It is further stressed that this kind of diet is both healthy and convenient, and is regarded as an important first step in the transition from meat to non-meat food.

Lacto-vegetarians: Many vegetarians (called "lacto-vegetarians") abstain from eggs, but consume milk and other dairy products like butter, cheese, ice cream and yogurt. One of the main rationales for adopting this diet is that one can easily get all of the essential nutrients-including calcium, iron, protein, vitamin D and vitamin B-12 as a lacto vegetarian.

Vegans: Pure vegetarians (or vegans) eat only foods of plant origin. Advocates of ethical vegetarianism argue that a lacto-ovo-vegetarian diet involves animal exploitation from battery farming methods. They also call attention to the close link between the meat-packers and the dairy farmers, and the fact that one group could not survive without the other.

A cow, for example, can only supply large amounts of milk when she has mothered a calf, so the dairy farmer makes certain that the cow gives birth to a calf on a regular basis. According to *American Dairyman,* most calves are taken from their mothers after their first day of life, and are fed a special artificial formula while their mothers' milk is taken for human consumption. The male calf is then raised for veal, or is used by the meat industry as a heifer or bull. The female is usually placed on the dairy line, and will be permitted to live until her production slackens. It is estimated that dairy cows, along with some 2.5 million bull calves, supply 18 per cent of all the beef consumed by humans in the United States. Much of the meat from cows - as well as their byproducts - are used by the commercial pet food industry.

Vegans also cite the conditions of the modem henhouse, which were described earlier in this chapter. Since overcrowding in henhouses often produces cannibalism, most laying hens are debeaked, and in order to reduce stress, sunlight is not permitted to enter the henhouse. To decrease the number of deaths that result from these unnatural conditions, the owners administer a wide variety of tranquilizers, hormones and antibiotics. After several months, the stressful conditions and the drugs begin to take their toll. When egg production slackens, the hen is killed and its meat is usually destined to be the main ingredient in commercial chicken soup, chicken pot pie or pet food.

Becoming a Vegetarian

For an aspirant to a life of ahimsa, a vegan diet is the most consistent with ethical considerations, though it may be somewhat difficult at first. Like any change in dietary habits, adopting a vegan diet should be in harmony with one's own capabilities, lifestyle and personal goals.

Many people have misconceptions about vegetarianism, and envision a diet without meat as being dull and repetitive. Since most meat-eaters are brought up on a menu that features a main course of meat sharing the platter with two overcooked vegetables, their negative feelings about a diet without meat are easy to understand.

For this reason, most new vegetarians have to rethink their concept of what constitutes a "typical" meal. By so doing, they open themselves up to a surprising variety of tasty main dishes composed of fresh vegetables and fruits, nuts, seeds, grains, pulses and sprouts. Many traditional foods of South and East Asia, The Mediterranean, the Middle East and Latin America involve no meat whatsoever, and are often simple and relatively inexpensive to prepare. A wide variety of casseroles, loaves, dips, soups, salads, sandwiches, stir-fried dishes, exotic cereals, and a broad range of wholegrain breads and pastries are enjoyed by vegetarians, and can be prepared by anyone with either a little imagination or a good vegetarian cookbook.

The psychological transition from a meat-dominated lifestyle to vegetarian fare may not appear easy at first, but after having experienced the variety of new dishes to choose from, many wonder why it was difficult to imagine a diet without meat.

Can a Vegetarian be Well-Nourished?

One of the major concerns confronting would-be vegetarians is whether they can be healthy and well-nourished on a meat-free diet. This fear was put to rest some years ago after the United States National Academy of Sciences came out in favor of vegetarian diets, and offered the following simple guidelines for proper vegetarian nutrition:

> As with all human diets, vegetarian diets should not contain excessive amounts of 'calories only' foods such as those containing chiefly starch, sugars, refined fats and oils, or alcohol. Two daily servings of high-protein meat alternates such as legumes, high-protein nuts, peanut butter, meat analogs, dairy products, or eggs are recommended. If dairy products are not used, calcium and riboflavin can be obtained in adequate amounts by liberal intake of dark green, leafy vegetables or by consumption of fortified soy milk. A vegetarian can be well nourished if he eats a variety of plant foods and gives attention to the critical nutrients mentioned above.

Some vegan diets may not contain adequate amounts of vitamin B-12, as very few non-animal foods are known to contain this nutrient. For this reason, most nutritionists advise vegans to take B-12 supplements which are derived from a special yeast culture easily available in tablet form, or consume soy products that are enriched with vitamin B-12. However, critics note that many vegans never develop a vitamin B-12 deficiency because it is excreted daily in bile and reabsorbed by the intestine. In addition, minute amounts of this vitamin can be found in sprouts, sea vegetables, tempeh (a soy derivative) and brewer's yeast.

Adopting a vegetarian lifestyle is not a difficult task. There are dozens vegetarian guidebooks and literally hundreds of vegetarian recipe books available that can help a potential vegetarian create a dietary plan that provides both sound nutrition and a variety of interesting menu plans. In addition, there are over a hundred vegetarian cookbooks on the market which show how meat-free meals can be exciting, delicious and easy to prepare. A partial listing of vegetarian literature and vegetarian organizations is included in Appendix II.

Why Else Vegetarianism?

In addition to its impact on animal welfare, a vegetarian lifestyle offers additional "ahimsic benefits" towards one's body, the environment, and the right utilization of the Earth's resources. Because a plant-based diet is naturally low in cholesterol and saturated fat, it is often recommended for those with high cholesterol and hypertension. And by getting off the top of the food chain, a vegetarian is subject to much lower pesticide residues than a meat- eater is. This low rate of pesticide ingestion and the elimination of the residues from the numerous drugs and hormones given to livestock has been cited as a factor for the lower cancer rates among vegetarians.

The practice of feeding plant protein to livestock instead of directly to people places a tremendous strain on the earth's resources, and contributes to the shortage of food around the world. The current annual cereal grain production is approximately 2,400 million tons, and if this amount were distributed among the 7.4 billion people in the world, each person would be provided with 50 per cent more grain than the estimated minimum needed to sustain life. The current practice of feeding grain to animals which indirectly convert it to meat severely accentuates the gap between those who are well fed and those who starve. The average American, for example, consumes nearly a ton of grain a year, although only 150 pounds are consumed directly as bread, cereal and pastry. The average Indian, Chinese or Colombian consumes only 350 pounds of grain a year.

According to David Pimentel, Emeritus Professor of Ecology at Cornell University's College of Agriculture and Life Sciences, "If all the grain currently fed to livestock in the United States were consumed directly by people, the number of people who could be fed would be nearly 800 million." In addition, a vegetarian diet calls for far less water than a diet containing meat. In a speech given at the Canadian Society of Animal Science in Montreal in 1997, Dr. Pimentel noted that grain-fed beef production takes 100,000 liters of water for every kilogram of meat. Raising broiler chickens takes 3,500 liters of water to make a kilogram of meat. In comparison, soybean production uses 2,000 liters for kilogram of food produced; rice, 1,912; wheat, 900; and potatoes, 500 liters.

According to Dr. Aaron Altschul of Georgetown University in Washington, the traditional mixed meat and plant diet popular in countries like Great Britain and the United States, utilizes some 2,500 gallons of water per person per day (including irrigation, animal drinking water, and the large amount of water needed for the actual processing of meat), while the pure vegetarian (vegan) diet uses only 300 gallons per day. The requirements of a lacto-vegetarian or lacto-ovo-vegetarian diet are estimated to lie somewhere between these extremes.

What about Honey?

According to the *Codex Alimentarius* – or Food Code- developed by United National Food and Agriculture Organization (FAO):

> Honey is the natural sweet substance
> produced by honey bees from the nectar of
> plants or from secretions of living parts of
> plants or excretions of plant sucking insects
> on the living parts of plants, which the bees
> collect, transform by combining with specific
> substances of their own, deposit, dehydrate,
> store and leave in the honey comb to ripen
> and mature.

Humans have been using honey as both food and medicine since about 15,000 B.C., but it wasn't until the 20th century that people turned bees into factory-farmed animals like cows, pigs and chickens. While there are still many small-scale beekeepers who treat their bees with care and respect, the vast majority are corporate beekeeping operations that use millions of bees.

There are many ethical issues involving the use of honey. Because bees are used to pollinate different crops in different areas of the country throughout the year, modern beekeeping involves transporting billions of bees over large distances, often resulting in stress and disease. They are also subjected to cold weather, drought, diseases (including those brought in by "guest" bees from abroad) and are poisoned by pesticides.

In years past, corporate beekeepers would kill the bees and take all the honey, but today's commercially-raised bees are not routinely killed but are often fed high-fructose corn syrup to compensate for the removal of honey from the hives. Poor nutrition takes a toll on their well-being, let alone their overall survival. For this reason, some who consume honey only focus on local and trusted beekeepers who take care of their bees. Many sell their honey at their farm stand or at farmers' markets.

Those who want to avoid honey can choose alternative sweeteners like rice syrup, molasses, sorghum, barley malt, maple syrup, cane sugar, and dried fruit or fruit concentrates.

However, an important point needs to be made: At the present time, more that 70 percent of the fruits and vegetables we eat – including carrots, cucumbers, broccoli, onions, pumpkins, squash, apples, blueberries, avocados and almonds- are pollinated by honeybees, and honey production is intimately connected to the pollination industry. Whether our diet includes meat or if we are strict vegans, our survival is intimately connected to bees and honey, along with the level of himsa that honey production involves.

What about Killing Plants?

One of the most common questions raised in the discussion of vegetarianism and ahimsa concerns the killing of plants for food. Studies have shown that plants sense that we are going to cut them, and tomatoes are said to scream when sliced.

It is a fact of life that our present stage of evolution calls for the eating of plants - either directly or indirectly - in order to survive. Until we are able to obtain our nutritional requirements directly from the sun, we will have to take our nutriment directly from the plant kingdom, thus doing the least amount of harm to sentient beings. As mentioned earlier, a vegetarian actually eats fewer plants than a meat-eater does, because the animal that the meat-eater has for dinner consumed thousands of pounds of plants in order to reach slaughter weight.

Advocates of ahimsa and vegetarianism point out that there is a vast amount of difference between the modest amount of himsa involved in obtaining the grains, fruits, vegetables and nuts that are essential for our survival, and the systematic slaughter of millions of animals every year which we can easily do without. H. Jay Dinshah, Founding President of the American Vegan Society, expanded on this point in the organization's magazine *Ahimsa:*

> To anyone who believes that life itself has some purpose - or is even its own reason for being - one should not wantonly destroy even plants. The destruction of any life is thus an act not to be taken lightly, or presumed to be isolated in the scheme of things. It is to be preceded with careful consideration of the responsibilities and the possible alternatives involved, and accompanied by an understanding that one is indeed doing the right thing according to his present state of existence . . . The ethical vegetarian is seriously interested in lessening the suffering that he may be causing in the world - even inadvertently inflicted upon relatively low forms of life.

One of the moral arguments against meat-eating is that we should allow - as much as possible - all beings to live out their natural life-cycles, thus affording them the opportunity to experience a full life, just as we do for ourselves. With this thought in mind, some vegetarians prefer to eat their fruits and vegetables only at the peak of ripeness, when the plant's cycle of life is complete.

Animal By-Products and Ahimsa

Although the ethical implications behind eating meat, eggs and dairy products are well known, a less obvious - and more controversial - issue involves the use of leather, wool and other "by-products" of the slaughterhouse. For many aspirants to a life of ahimsa, this is an exciting challenge, as the use of animal byproducts plays an important role in so many aspects of our daily existence.

Leather. Proponents of the use of leather state that since it is a natural by-product of the animal, obtaining it does not cause the animal's death. They maintain that leather is needed for human survival in many parts of the world, especially during the cold winter months, and that it represents the wise recycling of a natural resource.

Advocates of animal rights maintain that there is no such thing as an "innocent by-product", since the total commercial value of the animal includes the value of its hide. It is also cited that all byproducts help reduce the cost of meat, thus making it easier to obtain.

Advocates for animals point out that there are now many alternatives to leather shoes, including heavy canvas, hemp and imitation leather; in fact, some of the world's largest and style-conscious shoe companies now offer "vegan footwear". Other items, such as furniture coverings, belts, jackets, pocketbooks and other fashion accessories can be made from both natural and synthetic non-animal fibers.

Although the manufacture of synthetics often involves at least some degree of pollution to the environment, it is pointed out that animal rendering plants and tanneries are among the worst polluters in the industry. For this reason, clothing, shoes and other fashion accessories made from plants- especially cotton, hemp and bamboo - are often recommended as among least himsic products available today.

In India, leather is available from animals which have died a natural death, and many people there have chosen this source of leather over that from slaughtered animals. In China, people are often protected against the cold by heavy and durable quilted cotton coats. Some who use leather prefer to use only recycled products, and buy their shoes, belts and other leather items from second-hand stores because they do not feel directly responsible for creating the demand for leather.

Wool. The use of wool is also defended on the grounds that it is a natural product and does not directly involve the death of the animal. In most cases, the sheep which supply wool are not slaughtered for meat after the first shearing, although some 40 per cent of sheep and lambs are. The availability and cost of wool are dependent on the demand for meat from lambs and sheep, and those who use wool are indirectly involved in the slaughtering process.

Over the years many products have been developed to replace wool, such as heavy cotton, linen, ramie, polyester and other synthetics. Cotton flannel has long been used by people who have been allergic to wool, and coats made of cotton corduroy with synthetic linings have proven to be very effective against the cold. For other clothing, such as dresses, shirts, jackets and sweaters, cotton, hemp, bamboo or ramie are recommended as the natural fiber of choice. Although growing cotton often involves the heavy use of pesticides, it is said to involve less environmental pollution than the manufacture of synthetics.

Feathers. Most of the feathers used today are a by-product of chicken slaughter, and they are used primarily in stuffing. The most visible use of feathers, however, is in products made of goose down, such as sleeping bags, coats and quilts. Although the goose does not die from being plucked, the forced removal of its feathers is done in preparation for slaughter. Over the years, a wide variety of synthetic fibers have been developed which rival down for its lightness, durability and protection from the cold, and can be found in many products where down is traditionally used.

According to meat industry sources, many animal by-products are used in the manufacture of dozens of consumer items which are considered essential to daily life. Unfortunately, many of these products are "hidden" and are rarely detected except by the most aware consumers. In addition to the more obvious items like leather clothing, seat covers and fashion accessories, *animal hides* are used primarily in the manufacture of glue.

Bones, horns and hooves are used in the manufacture of gelatin, which can be found in desserts, marshmallows, and some ice creams and confectionery. It is also used in film, medicines and vitamin capsules. Bones alone are utilized in a wide variety of products, including buttons, piano keys and electrical bushings. Bone charcoal is often used to filter sugar cane.

Intestines and catgut are made into sausage casings, music strings and tennis racket strings. Most cheeses are coagulated with an enzyme taken from the intestines of calves and baby pigs, known as rennet. Some progressive and kosher dairies now use non-animal coagulants. Write to the dairy for specific information. Many supermarkets now sell rennet-free cheese and cheese made with vegetable rennet at little more than the price of other cheeses.

Hair is made primarily into brushes, rug pads and padding for furniture, while *blood* is used in cattle feed, fertilizer, pet foods and pharmaceuticals.

Animal fats and *glycerin* are often utilized in commercially prepared baked goods, such as biscuits and pastry. They are also used in the manufacture of glue, detergents, soap, shaving cream and cosmetics.

Some of these hidden animal products are impossible to avoid in today's society. While you can probably detect the presence of many ingredients of animal origin by carefully reading the product label, some ingredients are simply not listed by the manufacturer. You may be able to detect the presence of glycerin in suntan lotion or shaving cream from the label, but car tires do not carry a label mentioning that slaughterhouse by-products were used in their manufacture.

As Mahatma Gandhi pointed out many times throughout his life, we strive to attain ahimsa in a world of himsa, and it is impossible to avoid causing harm to other life-forms at our present stage of development. He believed we could best use our talents and energy towards working to avoid animal suffering while we live in the day-to-day world, as it is better to do some good than to withdraw from the world completely. As a vegetarian activist in California stated: "I would not avoid going to a vegetarian or animal rights rally because I was going to get there by rolling on tires down asphalt."

By changing one's diet to one limiting or avoiding animal products, we take a major step towards eliminating cruelty to animals. By purchasing clothing and fashion accessories from non-animal sources, we take another step towards compassion. And by carefully choosing cosmetics, soaps, nutritional supplements, quilts and other products that are free of animal by-products, we deepen our personal commitment to animal rights and ahimsa.

Chapter 8

Animals for Experimentation

*My view springs out of my non-violence,
for my soul rebels against vivisection . . .
Why should I have to practice cruelty on lower
animals which I would never practice on myself?*

-Mahatma Gandhi

THE TERM *VIVISECTION* COMES from the Latin word *vivus*, alive, and *sectio* from *secare*, to cut. Until recently, vivisection was limited only to "cutting up" living animals for purposes of research, although the term now includes any laboratory work which involves their suffering and/or death.

The subject of vivisection is a controversial one, even among students of ahimsa, and its arguments, both for and against, are often highly charged with emotion.

135

Whenever people point out the suffering involved in animal experiments - or even question their necessity - they are confronted with the argument "Oh, are you against a cure for cancer?" or "Would you rather have an intern practice on *people*?"

The prevailing belief among both orthodox scientists and the general public is that vivisection is the best research method available at this time which can find a cure for disease, test new chemicals and drugs, and help us to better understand certain aspects of human psychology. It is often pointed out that if animals were no longer used in this research, it would be necessary to experiment on human beings, just like Hitler's scientists did with the Jews during World War II. These arguments, along with a strong political lobby of physicians, drug manufacturers, research institutes, animal breeders, feed producers, case equipment manufacturers, shippers and brokers, have enabled the vivisection industry to grow tremendously over the years with government support.

Vivisection: the Basics

It has been estimated that between 100 million and 200 million animals die in laboratories around the world each year. According to the United States Department of Agriculture, American researchers use approximately 770,000 animals in research, testing, teaching and/or experimentation every year. However these do not include rats, mice, birds, reptiles, amphibians, and agricultural animals used in agricultural experiments), plus an estimated 100 million mice and rats used for other purposes. The number of animals used in other industrialized nations like Great Britain, France, Russia and Canada is believed to be proportionate to those used in the United States. Animals are primarily utilized in biomedical research, cognitive-behavior research, product development, drug testing, military research, space research and agricultural research.

Laboratory animals come from a number of sources. Primates are either captured in their native habitat and shipped to laboratories, or are specially bred domestically for laboratory use. Many cats and dogs are specially bred as well, although some come from animal shelters. This has caused an uproar among animal lovers, because recently captured pets are sometimes sold for research purposes before their owners can find them. Most other laboratory animals, such as mice, rabbits and guinea pigs, are bred for the purposes of vivisection.

Necessary and Proper?

Advocates of vivisection reform have estimated that perhaps 15 per cent of animal experimentation is "necessary and proper"' for the prevention and cure of disease. *Necessary* has been defined as "no alternative" while *proper* denotes "with every regard to the least suffering, wasteful loss of life and a choice of animals in regard to those least likely to suffer". An additional 15 per cent of animal experiments deal with other forms of medical research which fall outside the realm of "necessary and proper".

The remaining 70 per cent can be divided into the following largely non-medical areas:
1.   Environmental testing: Animals are used to help determine levels of toxins and other pollutants on a regular basis.
2.   Military testing: Research on the physical and psychological effects of nerve gas, napalm and other materials used in chemical and biological warfare. Studies are designed to evaluate the effects of exposure to radiation and other physical and psychological war-related hazards.

3.   Testing nonhumans for human habits: Research in drug addiction, cigarette smoking, and alcohol dependency.

4.   Psychological testing: Utilizing nonhumans in tests claimed to be of use to people. Such testing often involves prolonged isolation, as well as physical and psychological torture.

5.   Product testing: Laboratory animals are widely used to test cosmetics, shampoos, detergents and other products in order to determine their harmful effects on people.

6.   Scientific tinkering: Research undertaken, often at public expense, to satisfy the curiosity of certain scientists.

7.   Repeating old experiments because the researcher did not check published literature.

8.   Repeating old experiments in order to teach: Such experiments are regularly conducted in high schools and colleges (especially in medical schools) where students perform surgery, amputations, and work with electrodes. Additional vivisection is done for extra-credit projects at high school science fairs.

Types of Vivisection

Vivisection takes many forms, and is performed either with or without anesthesia. The major categories of animal experiments are described in brief below.

Toxicological experiments. These involve using animals to determine the acute and chronic toxicities of new chemical compounds. They often involve subjecting animals to electric shock and burning in order to test new lotions and salves. Animals are induced to stressful conditions in the testing of sedatives, and cosmetics are applied to exposed skin and eyes to test for irritation. Animals are infected with certain diseases in order to test new drugs. Many of these experiments are performed without anesthetics, such as the Draize test, which involves placing chemical compounds directly into the eyes of rabbits to determine toxicity.

Pain and stress. These experiments involve withholding postoperative painkillers in order to observe psychological responses. Painful electric shocks to the brain are given, both for observing psychological reactions, and in conditioning the animals to respond to various stimuli.

Prep-killing and fighting experiments. This type of research calls for the mutilation of a predator to study the effect on its aggressive behavior towards comparatively defenseless smaller animals. Castration, cutting of olfactory nerves (that regulate the ability to smell) and electric shock through metal grids or electrodes planted in the brain are often used to stimulate aggression and prey-killing. The results of these tests, which are often performed on monkeys, cats and rodents, are claimed to be valuable for better understanding the behavior of humans.
Radiation. Both mild and severe doses of radiation are administered to the animal in order to determine danger levels. Radiation is also used to study the physical effects of rodents, dogs and monkeys suffering from induced cancers. Many of the radiation experiments are government-funded. After the partial meltdown of the nuclear reactor near Chernobyl in Ukraine, laboratory research on animals' response to radiation increased substantially.

Surgical experiments. These involve experimental burns, parabiosis (the surgical joining of two individuals), and "practice" or demonstration surgery, performed primarily on dogs. Other experiments study the effect of surgical manipulation of animals, such as mutilating the sex organs of cats in order to observe changes in their mating habits.

Battering experiments. Battering includes beating or crushing of an animal's limbs, and inducing shock by battering a non-anaesthetized animal in a revolving drum. It also involves "skull smashing" in testing football helmets and in determining the safety of motor vehicles in violent crashes.

Vivisection: Reform or Abolition?

By its very nature, vivisection involves the imprisonment, manipulation and injury of laboratory animals. During the past several years, a large volume of evidence has come to light revealing widespread neglect, callous treatment, and even sadism on the part of those who experiment on these creatures. The present status of laboratory animals has become a matter of deep concern to increasing numbers of humanitarians throughout the world.

Most individuals and animal welfare groups accept the theory that animal experimentation is necessary. For this reason their primary goal is to ensure that the laboratory animals are given the most humane treatment possible, and that they are used only in experiments that are deemed absolutely necessary. The basic thrust of their work is directed towards highlighting flagrant abuses, lobbying for more humane legislation regulating the use of laboratory animals, and the strict observation of these laws on a practical level. In addition, much work is being done to inform the public about certain aspects of vivisection in the form of literature, advertisements, workshops and educational films.

In the United States, the Animal Welfare Act became law in 2013, and provided guidelines for the transportation, sale and handling of certain animals. Though a step in the right direction, critics maintain that the AWA does not include rats, mice, fish and birds, which comprise around 95 percent of the animals used in scientific research.

Mahatma Gandhi and others have taught that the acceptance of vivisection - whether humane or otherwise - is both cruel and futile. They maintain that despite the high increase in animal experimentation over the years, there is more disease than ever before.

Doubts regarding the usefulness of vivisection are shared by scientists, who point out that the results of laboratory experiments on rabbits, rodents, dogs or monkeys are often not applicable to human beings. It was reported that during a recent year, 94 percent of drugs that passed animal tests failed in human trials. A 2013 study published in the *Archives of Toxicology* stated that "The low predictivity of animal experiments in research areas allowing direct comparisons of mouse versus human data puts strong doubt on the usefulness of animal data as key technology to predict human safety."

Abolitionists like Gandhi, while accepting that efforts to ensure the humane treatment of laboratory animals may have a sincere motive, believe that the humane philosophy is similar to that of the pre-Civil War reformers in the United States who called for better working and living conditions for slaves. They also believe that humane groups add respectability to the business of animal experimentation, and soothe the conscience of those who benefit from it.

Although they support reform their ultimate goal is the complete abolition of animal experimentation. Alex Pacheco, cofounder of People for the Ethical Treatment of Animals (PETA) wrote:

Realizing that total abolition of some aspects
of animal exploitation may never come, we
should not simply demand 'total abolition or

nothing at all', as that often ensures that those suffering today will continue to suffer. Nor should we hold a conservative line which will also make tomorrow's suffering assured and accepted . . . We must fight for today's reforms while aiming for and advocating abolition.

Alternatives to Vivisection

In place of animal experimentation, abolitionists and others have drawn attention to many of the sophisticated modern methods presently available that do not involve the use of animals. In addition, they support channeling research money towards developing and refining other alternatives to vivisection that do not involve the imprisonment, pain or suffering of laboratory animals.

At the present time, a number of viable alternatives to vivisection are available, and their increased use could greatly reduce animal suffering in the world. They include:

1.   Tissue cultures / in vitro testing: These can be obtained from humans with no risk and little discomfort. Tissue cultures can be used in cancer research, radiation testing, smoking experiments, and in the testing of drugs and cosmetics. The use of human diploid culture cells has proven to be effective in the testing and manufacture of certain vaccines that formerly were extracted from monkeys and other animals. Human cells can now be grown to mimic the structure and function of human organs and organ systems.

2.   Human organs: Removed in the normal course of surgery or after death, organs such as the heart, liver, stomach, skin and eyes could be effectively used in place of

live animals. They could be widely utilized to test new chemicals, drugs, the effects of radiation, stress and other aspects of biological research.

3.   Dummies: Mechanical models, mathematical models, humanoid dummies and human cadavers could be utilized in battering and crash experiments. Recently developed computerized human – patient simulators can breathe, bleed, talk and even die, and are becoming widely used in student training.

4.   Computer simulation and computer modeling: This development can sharpen the accuracy of research and can dramatically reduce the number of experiments needed for a given project.

5.   Models and films: Detailed models of animals are available for high school and college teaching. The use of video for instruction can be highly effective and can dramatically reduce the number of animals used in the classroom or laboratory.

6.   Careful use of literature: This can avoid the senseless repetition of animal experiments which have already yielded the necessary information.

7.   Research with human volunteers, especially in behavior research and drug testing. This can often include "microdosing" and using advanced brain imaging and recording techniques. Human volunteers are also frequently used in evaluating experimental drugs and in clinical trials for medical procedures.

Because biomedical research, safety testing and medical education are conducted primarily for the benefit of humans, some advocates of animal rights have proposed the highly controversial alternative of utilizing brain-dead humans (whose physiological functions - such as breathing - are maintained by artificial means) for biomedical testing and research.

Such special cadavers (known as "neomorts") are considered both medically and legally dead. However, since they resemble comatose patients who breathe, require nourishment and eliminate waste, they are also physically alive but are believed to feel no pain.

Potential uses of brain-dead humans include medical education (such as practicing difficult diagnostic and surgical procedures), toxicity testing, research (such as the development of cures after experimentally induced illness and discovering effective drugs), the storage of specialized blood components and transplantable organs, the harvesting of bone marrow, skin and cartilage, and the manufacture of hormones, antitoxins, antibodies and other elements.

Although eminently practical, the suggestion of using neomorts for biomedical research and education brings up many sensitive - and important - ethical and religious issues. However, organ retrieval for transplantation was also considered radical years ago, yet it is endorsed by major philosophers and religious groups today. Because the use of neomorts can eventually reduce animal suffering, it is worthy of further consideration and discussion.

Towards Ending Vivisection

Until people begin to make a sincere commitment to speaking out against painful experiments on animals, vivisection will continue. Elinor Seiling, the founder of the American group United Action for Animals, believed that the main focus for changing national policies on vivisection should be in the legislature which has sanctioned the practice of vivisection by law. She also stressed the need for education regarding the nature and goals of much humane legislation, which is often designed to promote the practice of animal experimentation instead of reducing it. She pointed out that many new statutes call for alternatives to be applied *in addition* to the traditional cruel methods rather than *in place* of them.

In addition to applying pressure on elected representatives and new candidates for political office, there is much the individual can do to help reduce and eliminate vivisection. One of the most important aspects of this work is to become educated in the basic issues surrounding animal experimentation: speciesism, uncontrolled breeding of dogs and cats, reform versus abolition, and alternatives to animal research. Individuals can find out where, how, and what kind of animal experiments are being carried out at local schools, zoos and in government and private research facilities, and present their findings to the public. People can picket laboratories that perform such experiments and urge their cessation, while working to help change laws that promote them.

Students at both the high school and university levels can refuse to experiment on animals and insist on utilizing available alternatives instead. Parents can take an active role in abolishing animal experiments in schools, and in educating children on the major issues of animal rights and human obligations towards their welfare.

Some have chosen more radical action. Members of groups like the Animal Liberation Front have broken into research laboratories where animal experiments are performed. After photographs and/or movies are taken of the animals and the conditions in the laboratory, the animals are liberated from the premises and the instruments of torture are often destroyed. The media is then contacted and by the following morning, millions of people become aware of the realities of animal experiments in their midst. In one such case near Washington D.C., the director of the laboratory was eventually tried and convicted in court for neglect of the animals in his lab.

Because some feel that the destruction of property is not an act of ahimsa, laboratory break-ins and vandalism are discouraged. They also cite the possibility that human beings already in the building may be inadvertently killed or injured during the incursion.

Others believe that the protection of other living beings is the highest goal of ahimsa. They feel that these dramatic efforts have helped focus public attention on the realities of animal suffering in the laboratory, and will stimulate the movement towards finding animal-free alternatives.

Some Personal Strategies

There are other more personal methods to help eliminate vivisection.

1. Take the "Cruelty Free Pledge" and buy only products (especially soaps, hair care products, lotions and cosmetics) that do not involve animal testing. At the time of this writing, over two thousand companies are offering products that are not tested on animals. A database of these companies is available on PETA's web site, and they deserve consumer support.

2. Consumers can boycott the myriad of new products - such as pills, shampoos, detergents, cosmetics and food additives – that are constantly being imposed on them by manufacturers and which all require extensive animal testing. Letters can be sent to the customer service departments of the manufacturers explaining the reasons

behind the boycott (a copy of the letter can be sent to the local newspaper as well).

3. Another major way to reduce our personal involvement with animal exploitation is to consciously maintain our health through preventive health care. This will not only make us feel better, but will lessen our dependency on doctors and drugs. Chronic diseases, such as heart disease, cancer, and diabetes, are responsible for 7 of every 10 deaths among Americans each year and account for 75 percent of the nation's health spending. We can also insist that the government increase research spending on preventive health care, rather than devote most of its research funds to "sickness care" as is presently being done.

4. Finally, educate friends, family and colleagues about vivisection and its alternatives.

For a student of ahimsa, the problem of animal experimentation is a very serious one. Much study and deep reflection is needed for achieving a truly ethical orientation. Should nonhumans be used to dispel the ignorance that humans have about health and disease? Is vivisection justifiable under any circumstances? If animal experiments were to cease, would it bring about more human suffering and death? Where should the emphasis lie: reform or abolition? If vivisection were abolished, would a more intensified effort be made to find alternatives, or would new and future discoveries suffer as a result?

Chapter 9

Animals for Sport,
Animals for Fur

All beings are fond of themselves, they like pleasure,
they hate pain, they shun destruction,
they like life and want to live long.
To all, life is dear; hence their life should be protected.

-Lord Mahavira

FOR THE MILLIONS OF YEARS that preceded *Homo sapiens'* appearance on Earth, a state of relative equilibrium existed among the inhabitants of the planet. Species appeared, thrived, evolved and disappeared according to a well-established life-cycle, often accompanied by powerful earth changes, such as earthquakes, floods, climate change and volcanic eruptions. Even after our early ancestors began walking the earth many thousands of years ago, a natural state of equilibrium continued to exist as they eked out a living in an often hostile environment. Early *Homo sapiens* gathered seeds and nuts and occasionally killed other animals for food, clothing and shelter. However, since humans were few in number and their weapons primitive, the overall impact on the natural environment was relatively small.

As humans developed more sophisticated weapons and better methods of self-defense, the number of animals they killed sharply increased. However, the majority of animals they killed were still used primarily to ensure their survival in an often hostile world. In many cultures, the killing of animals was regulated by tribal law, and was treated as a very serious matter. Many indigenous peoples from around the world continue to respect the Earth's natural balance. Although they may kill animals for food or clothing, they do so only for what they consider to be legitimate survival needs. The idea of hunting or trapping animals for pleasure or to acquire trophies or souvenirs is incomprehensible to them.

The roots of modern-day hunting probably began with the advent of firearms in the fifteenth century. Killing animals for reasons of self-defense or food became secondary, and killing animals for pleasure became more widespread. The extremes of this attitude were revealed in the American West, where millions of bison that peacefully inhabited the Great Plains were mercilessly shot for the pleasure of killing them. Native Americans used every part of the bison. In addition to food, the bison provided tipis and clothing made from hides to soap from fat and tools made from bones. As a result, bison were honored as relatives and paid tribute to through songs, dance and prayers. The wholesale slaughter of bison not only nearly exterminated a species, but deprived many Native Americans of their major source of food, shelter and clothing. As a result, many of them died.

The killing of animals for sport, for pleasure, for excitement and human vanity is of great concern to aspirants to a life of ahimsa. While a relatively small minority of people in the United States (approximately 5 percent of adults over the age of 16) actually hunt, and trap, they are responsible for the suffering and death of over 100 million animals every year, which does not include the millions of animal deaths not reported to state agencies. The majority of animals that are hunted and trapped every year in North America include bear, caribou, moose, antelope, elk, deer, waterfowl, rabbits, squirrels and upland birds. Hunting is a big business in the Unites States, with annual expenditures of approximately $34 billion a year.

Because hunting and trapping are respected institutions whose roots extend back hundreds of years in our society, those who object to them are viewed as unpatriotic "bleeding hearts" who are out of touch with the reality of the wilds. However, given the tremendous amount of animal suffering through hunting and trapping, as well as the large amount of taxpayer's money that sustains a vast pro-hunting and trapping "conservation/wildlife management" structure, the need for education and individual action is especially needed at this time. In the following pages we will briefly examine some of the major issues surrounding hunting, trapping and raising animals for fur, and we will explore some of the more ahimsic avenues of personal commitment and action.

Hunting

It has been estimated that there are over 12.5 million hunters in the United States over the age of sixteen. Unlike their ancestors, today's hunter is often equipped with a high-powered rifle with a telescopic sight. He (hunting still seems to appeal mostly to men: only 9 percent of American hunters are female) is often transported to the hunting area by car, motorbike or a four- wheeled drive vehicle, thus making even the remotest natural areas accessible. Some use hunting dogs, two-way radios and even helicopters to help ensure their success in the wilds.

Although deer, rabbits, duck and pheasant make up the most popular "game" animals in North America, the fox hunt remains a venerable British tradition, although hunting with dogs was banned in the United Kingdom in 2005. In the United States and Canada, nearly everything else that moves is sought by hunters, including bear, antelope, beaver, moose, wolves, quail, geese, doves, badgers, mountain lions and wild goats.

"Canned Hunting"

Many are killed through so-called "canned hunting" where animals – including surplus animals from zoos and animals bred to be hunted- are placed in a confined area from which they cannot escape. The victims are usually exotic (non-indigenous) species, including several varieties of goats and sheep; numerous species of Asian and African antelope; deer, cattle, and swine. They can also include bears, zebra, and sometimes even big cats. Although a handful of U.S. states prohibit hunting animals in enclosures, there are over a thousand canned hunting operations in some twenty-five states.

Trophy Hunting

Exotic animals have long been the targets of hunters as well, and those who can afford to travel to Africa on safari can hunt antelope, zebras, giraffes and lions. Delaware Action for Animals estimates that tens of thousands of wild animals, representing hundreds of different species, are killed by American trophy hunters in foreign countries each year, mostly in Africa. The heads, hides, tusks, and other body parts of most of these animals are then legally imported to the United States by the hunters or their agents.

In 2015, the killing of Cecil, a beloved lion that was lured from Zimbabwe's Hwang National Park and killed by a Minnesota dentist who paid $55,000 for the privilege, generated a chorus of outrage around the world. The shooter's main regret was that he was not aware that Cecil was a famous lion. He also felt sorry that was not aware that Cecil was part of an ongoing research study with Oxford University. The shooter was a member of Safari Club International, a hunter's rights organization that proudly listed the dentist's 43 other trophy kills on its website, including a polar bear.

However, as so-called "wildlife preserves" proliferate in North America, American and Canadian hunters can shoot such exotica as Sika deer, Ibex goat, bison, elk, and Mouflon ram for a price without having to travel to Africa.

Why Hunting?

There are several arguments which modem hunters use to legitimize their killing of animals in the wild. These are listed below.

The Hunter as Nature Lover. It is somewhat difficult to understand why a lover of Nature and Her creatures would spend his or her time and money to kill them. According to James Madson of the Olin Matheison gun company:

> The hunter often deludes himself and buries
> his motives. Yet, his ultimate motive in
> hunting is to kill. All other reasons, however
> important, are secondary. Remove the

conscious intention of shooting something
and a hunt is simply a walk in the country.

The Hunter as Ecologist. The term "wildlife conservation" has long been the crux of the pro-hunting argument. Long-established and well-funded departments of conservation have been active on state and national levels to ensure that hunters always have an adequate amount of animals to shoot, thus maintaining the "balance of nature" by saving thousands of animals from starvation.

In many cases, natural predators have been exterminated so that game animals, like deer, will multiply. Local and national government agencies are not alone in promoting hunting for the sake of ecology and wildlife management. The hunting industry itself has a tremendous stake in the continued sales of guns, ammunition, bows and arrows and other equipment. These pro-hunting forces have organized into a variety of rifle associations, animal conservation groups, and wildlife federations that work to promote and protect the hunters' way of life. Despite their campaign to convince the public that hunting is done primarily for ecological balance and the animals' well-being, certain points demand clarification:

1.	The trophy hunter does not kill as natural predators do. While natural predators go after sick, old and weaker animals, the hunter seeks out the very best. As a result, the long-term potential of a "conserved" species is diminished, because animals with the best genes are destroyed.
2.	Hunters maintain that shooting an animal is more humane than a slow and painful death from starvation. They rarely mention that hundreds of thousands of game animals are left wounded by hunters, as well as the countless other animals which are killed by "mistake".
3.	The major reason for overpopulation of certain animals is that humans have systematically destroyed their

natural predators, such as the fox, eagle, wolf and coyote. This has upset the delicate balance which Nature has perfected over thousands, if not millions, of years. The destruction of predatory animals is often orchestrated by various wildlife management programs specifically designed to bring about a surplus of a species, thus giving the hunters an excuse to 'save' them from suffering and starvation. According to Cleveland Amory in *Man Kind?*:

> Man has an infinite capacity to rationalize his own cruelty. The reason why there are too many rabbits is that the hunters, however much they love potting at rabbits and squirrels and woodchucks and chipmunks and virtually everything that moves, like even better potting bigger and better things - such as all the animals of which the rabbit are the natural prey, and which the hunters have shot off to virtual extinction.

Instead of compounding an unnatural situation, advocates of animal rights suggest that the reintroduction of predatory animals into the forests would be a good solution to the problem of overpopulation of certain species. In addition, if the present expansion of human civilization (whether for sport, housing construction or lumbering) were curbed, natural predators would be better able to survive in the wild and help bring back a natural balance of predator/prey which humans have disrupted over the years.

The Hunter as Sportsman. It has been pointed out that there is no "sport" as long as one of the participants is armed and the other is both defenseless and unaware that a contest is taking place. According to the Ethical Humanist leader Saul K. Padover, "If the hunted were equipped with the same powerful and often expensive weapons as the two-legged hunter, and could be taught to use them, then hunting might be more sportsmanlike."

Some suggest that an exciting and peaceful alternative to hunting with a gun may be to "hunt" using a camera with a telephoto lens. Rather than use the split-second encounter to kill, the photographer can immortalize life.

Sport Hunters as Paying Their Way. Although vast amounts of revenues are taken in by government agencies for duck stamps, fishing licenses and hunting permits, most of the money used to finance wildlife management does not come from hunters. For example, during a recent year, the funds allocated to the Fish and Wildlife Service from the United States Department of the Interior amounted to $3 billion in 2017. Of this, just $1.3 million resulted from the sale of duck stamps, $110 million from taxes on fishing gear, and $900 million from excise taxes on firearms and ammunition (for all types of guns and ammunition, not just those used for hunting). The remaining $2 billion or 66 per cent came from general tax revenues, which means that the average non-hunting taxpayer pays an annual subsidy to support recreational hunting. Figures are similar for state wildlife management budgets, which devote the vast majority of their funds towards game (as opposed to nongame) animal management for the benefit of hunters.

Commercial Hunting and Fishing

In addition to sport hunting, many animals in the wild have been hunted and killed purely for their monetary value. Much has been written about the annual slaughter of baby harp seals in Labrador and the Pribilov Islands in Alaska, where these animals are clubbed to death in order to provide humans with coats and fashion accessories made from their soft, white fur. Killing animals for their fur will be discussed in greater detail later on in this chapter.

Attention also needs to be given to the destruction of sea animals for profit, such as whales and dolphins. After many years of tireless effort, the whale is finally becoming protected by international treaty, although their welfare requires constant monitoring by animal rights groups like Greenpeace and governmental agencies.

Dolphins are often killed in the process of netting tuna, which frequently swim with the dolphins on the high seas. Some feel that until an alternative method of netting tuna is developed which would not harm the dolphins, consumers should boycott the purchase of tuna, thus reducing demand.

Although such a proposal certainly has its merits, the underlying premise is inconsistent with ahimsa: animals which are of commercial or food value to humans should be killed, while those which have no commercial value should be protected, especially if they are intelligent and lovable like dolphins. From an ahimsic point of view, a more consistent argument would suggest that a permanent moratorium on tuna fishing would not only save the dolphins, but would also give tuna their natural right to a full life-cycle, just as we humans demand for ourselves.

Trapped and Farmed

The fur salon is often portrayed as the ultimate in civilized elegance and good taste. Thick carpeting, delicate chandeliers, gilt-edged mirrors and well-dressed, attentive salespeople all contribute to the image of affluence and luxury where furs are sold.

During the past few years, more and more people have started to look behind the genteel facade of the fur salon, and have begun to consider where these beautiful coats, stoles and hats actually came from. A mink or muskrat coat contains the skins of between sixty and seventy dead animals, and represents the sum total of considerable suffering and violent death.

Trapping, like hunting, is big business in many parts of the world, especially in northern countries like the United States, Canada, Norway, Finland and Russia. It is estimated that there are roughly 175,000 trappers in the United States alone. Of these, approximately one fifth consider trapping to be their major source of income. In addition, a large sector of the fur business is devoted to raising animals, such as mink, in captivity until they are slaughtered for their pelts. By 2014, sales of fur in the United States alone amounted to $1.5 billion, a figure that has been fairly constant since 1985. The number of animals killed for human fashion is estimated to be more than one billion rabbits and 50 million other animals - including foxes, seals, mink and dogs -are raised on fur farms or trapped in the wild and killed for their pelts.

In addition to the use of fur in traditional items such as women's coats, stoles and jackets, furs are now in vogue for men. The introduction of so-called "fun furs" have also been met with positive consumer reaction, as coyote bedspreads, wolf skin jackets, and muskrat-covered furniture have become increasingly popular among well-heeled consumers.

Here is a partial list of animals used for fur coats, jackets, hats, wraps and coverlets:

leopard	otter	lynx	red fox
seal	wolf	raccoon	mink
rabbit	squirrel	beaver	chinchilla
muskrat	bear	badger	broadtail lamb
martin	opossum	zebra	deer
coyote	buffalo	llama	moose

The following animals are also killed for clothing, fashion objects, toys and other consumer goods:

Alligator (shoes, wallets, handbags, souvenirs)
Antelope (purses, gloves, fashion accessories)
Kangaroo (fashion accessories, trophies, stuffed toys)
Wild goat (clothing, fashion accessories)
Civet cat (furs, perfume, musk oil)
Boar (clothing, bristle brushes, fashion items)
Monkey (furs, for testing cosmetics)
Elephant (ivory, trophies, fashion accessories)
Birds (feathers)
Rabbit (furs, souvenirs, for testing cosmetics)

Trapping

Many of the animals killed for fur are raised in captivity, and approximately 50 per cent of them are trapped. The most popular method of trapping is the leghold trap. Although first developed in the early nineteenth century, it has not changed substantially for almost two hundred years.

The leghold trap is deceptively simple, both in appearance and in actual operation. The basic trap consists of a piece of sprung steel and two semi-circular jaws. The jaws are forced open and a small piece of metal, known as the "dog", is placed across them, wedging its unattached end into a grooved shank of a flat metal dish known as the "pan".

The leghold trap is set either on the trail of an animal, in its burrow or den, or close to a "bait" or strong-smelling lure. When the animal steps on the pan, the 'dog' mechanism is released and the jaws snap shut on the animal's leg. A chain is attached to the trap, which is in turn securely fastened to a stake or tree. The animal is helplessly trapped until the trapper returns to kill it, several hours or even several days later. The trapper finally kills the animal by stomping it, clubbing it with a blunt instrument, or through strangulation.

The leghold trap

The pain and terror experienced by trapped animals is excruciating, and many have been known to chew off their own paws in order to regain their precious freedom. This is most common in the case of a nursing mother, who is apt to bite off a trapped paw immediately in order to return to her young.

The animal rights group Born Free USA estimates that some four million animals are trapped in the United States every year, while The Fur Institute in Canada estimates that approximately 750,000 animal pelts are "harvested" annually in Canada from traps. Exact statistics are difficult to come by, but most of these animals are killed with the leghold trap, mainly because it is cheap, effective and easy to use.

The animals most sought after by trappers in North America include the muskrat, nutria, wild mink, raccoon, fox, beaver, bobcat, badger, lynx, fisher, otter, martin, weasel, skunk, opossum, coyote, and ring-tailed cat. The least wanted animals are small birds, rabbits, small rodents and domestic dogs and cats. They are often referred to as "trash" by trappers, because their pelts have little or no commercial value. Of course large birds- including owls, hawks and bald eagles- are often accidently trapped by this method.

In view of the cruelty involved in the leghold trap, the outright banning of its use has long been a goal of humanitarians throughout the world. The leghold trap has been declared inhumane by the American Veterinary Medical Association, the American Animal Hospital Association, and the National Animal Control Association. Its use has been banned or severely restricted by more than one hundred countries and seven U.S. states.

A Humane Trap?

Over the years, much work has been done to develop a so-called "humane trap" that would reduce the animals' prolonged pain and suffering. Perhaps the most humane trap developed to date is the Havahart®, which traps the animal in a cage unharmed. However, this type of trap is mainly designed to catch smaller animals- such as squirrels, gophers and raccoons- and costs more eight to ten times more than the leghold trap, which can be purchased for under five dollars apiece.

Another alternative trap is the "instant kill" Conibear®, named after its inventor Victor Conibear. Unlike the leghold trap, the Conibear was designed to break the animal's neck and/or backbone, thus shutting off the flow of blood and oxygen to the brain. It consists of two square-shaped jaws designed to shut instantly when a spring mechanism is released. An animal walking into a Conibear trap has been compared to a human walking into a revolving door whose four partitions are cocked apart by powerful springs.

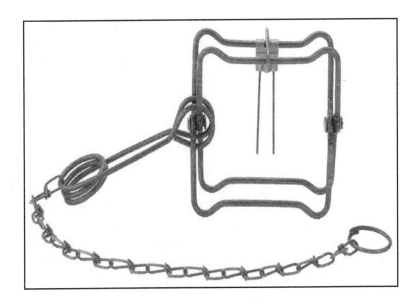

The Conibear trap

The main drawback to the Conibear trap, besides its higher price, is its tendency to be non-selective, and its ability to kill or maim any animal that touches it, regardless of size. If the animal is too large for the trap, the Conibear effect is similar to that of the leghold trap. It causes the trapped animal the same prolonged pain and terror it was designed to eliminate. Although newer designs are believed to be more efficient, traditional Conibear traps have been estimated to kill fewer than 15 percent of trapped animals quickly, and more than 40 percent of those trapped die slow, painful deaths as their abdomens, heads, or other body parts are crushed.

Like other efforts to reduce cruelty to animals, the subject of "humane trapping" is a highly controversial one. Humanitarians maintain that a humane trap is an important first step towards replacing the more brutal leghold trap.

Opponents say that whether the animal is trapped in a Conibear or leghold trap has little significance, because in the end it is just as dead. Abolitionists also maintain that the speciesist motivation behind trapping is the same no matter what methods are used, and that humane trapping serves as a cloak of respectability for pro-trapping advocates.

The rationale behind trapping is the same which the hunters use to defend hunting. When the cause of ecology became fashionable in the early 1970s, the fur industry and its suppliers - the trappers - embraced it eagerly. Since there are few natural predators left in the forest to maintain a natural balance of wildlife, the trapper claims to have a duty to 'harvest' the surplus. Like the hunter, the trapper has long been the major predator of the predators, whose near-extinction has been the primary cause for forest overpopulation.

In place of trapping, animal rights advocates call on humans to cease their encroachment on heavily forested and wilderness areas. The use of four-wheeled vehicles, track bikes and snowmobiles, housing construction, logging operations and other forms of disruption of the wild should end. The natural predators can be reintroduced into the region to help restore the natural balance of wildlife once more.

Ranch-raised Fur

According to fur industry sources, some 50-60 per cent of animals used for fur in the United States are ranch-raised. While exact statistics are difficult to come by, some 70 million mink and 3.7 million fox alone were killed for their pelts during a recent year. The countries that breed and kill the greatest numbers of mink include China, Denmark, Poland, the United States, Eastern Europe (excluding Poland) and Greece. Those which breed and kill the majority of foxes for their fur include Finland, China, Norway, Poland and Russia.

Although promoted by the industry as a more humane alternative to the evils of trapping, many animal rights advocates disagree. They point out that because there are no federal regulations regarding cage size, humane treatment or inspection of facilities, fur-bearing animals rarely receive the protection legally afforded to livestock killed for meat. Because the animals' flesh is not used for human consumption, there is no strong incentive to preserve their health and wellbeing.

Many fur-bearing animals are accustomed to movement and space, and forced confinement is a cause for severe stress throughout their lives in captivity. Finally, cruel slaughtering methods are often employed to kill ranch-raised animals. Strychnine, primitive electrocution and carbon monoxide gas are the preferred methods of killing.

Towards Restoring Balance

For a student of ahimsa, a deep personal understanding of both the short-term and long-term effects of killing animals for sport or human vanity is a top priority. The practices of hunting, trapping and ranching all involve cruelty and violence, and degrade the animal as an object to be used for recreation, vanity and profit. At the same time, the humans who inflict this cruelty on animals (either directly or by proxy) are degraded in turn as they trivialize the essential worth of other living beings and their right to enjoy a full life-cycle in their natural habitat.

The basic law of both conservation and ahimsa teaches that all forms of life are interdependent. The prey is as dependent on the natural predator to help control its population as the predator is on the prey for its supply of food. Nature has seen to this for millions of years, and many indigenous peoples throughout the world have respected this need for balance in nature. Modern industrialized society has, through greed and short-sightedness, profoundly upset this balance. With the knowledge that we have, we must work to restore this balance once again, and strive to make the planet's ecosystems stable once more. We need to rethink our outdated concept of 'conservation' without limiting our perspective to what may best suit special interest groups like hunters and trappers in the short term. We must begin to view ourselves as a part of the planetary ecosystem rather than apart from it.

For an advocate of ahimsa, there are many possibilities for both individual and group work in these areas of animal protection.

1.   Education. In order to do effective work, a solid grounding in the basic issues involving hunting, trapping and ranch-raising are necessary. Books like *Animal Liberation, The American Hunting Myth,* and magazines like *The Animals' Agenda* (see Appendix) are good sources of information.

2.   Inform others through schoolroom presentations and by sharing your beliefs through personal contact, public

forums, social media and letters to the editor of your local paper.

3.   Investigate the local wildlife councils, fish and game commissions, or boards of game in your local community. These quasi- governmental bodies are often composed of hunters and other pro-hunting people, and can often play a major role in making policy for state fish and game departments. Work with other animal rights activists to get appointed to these boards.

4.   If you live in a rural area, place "No Hunting" signs around your land and urge your neighbors to do the same.

5.   Join an anti-hunting group. These organizations are not only involved in educating the public, but stage demonstrations and other nonviolent actions to call attention to the cruelties of hunting and trapping. In addition to disrupting the duck hunt by blowing horns and playing loud music near duck blinds (hence chasing away the ducks before the hunters can shoot them) members of the U.S.-based Coalition to Abolish Sport Hunting visited old-age homes in the state of Massachusetts. Since many hunting licenses are available in limited numbers, they gave out applications for licenses to the elderly residents of these homes, who of course had no interest in hunting. As a result, the number of licenses available to hunters was sharply reduced, thus limiting the number of animals to be killed during hunting season.

6. Work for legislative change regarding laws on hunting and trapping. The active involvement of even a few well-educated citizens can have a powerful effect on the political process.

7. Join with your neighbors to preserve and protect

wooded areas, saving them from encroachment by housing developers.

8. Vow never to wear furs yourself and seek out non-animal alternatives.

9. Become involved with a group whose goal is to educate the public about the cruelties inherent in buying and wearing fur. These groups engage in public speaking, boycotts and demonstrations at stores that sell fur.

10. On a more personal level, we can develop a greater sensitivity towards animals in the forest through hiking, observation and photography. In many parts of the world, the financial contribution made by "wildlife watchers" is greater than that of hunters and trappers. In the United States during a recent year, some 21 million Americans participated in wildlife watching.

As we deepen our own contact with other animal species, we can learn how to be more responsible custodians of this planet who will nurture and protect the environment we share with other life forms.

Chapter 10

Animals for Entertainment and Companionship

For the animal shall not be measured by man. In a world older and more complete, gifted with extension of the senses we have lost or never attained, living by voices we shall never hear. They are not brethren, they are not underlings. They are other nations, caught with ourselves in the net of life and time, fellow prisoners of the splendor and travail of the earth.

-Henry Beston

IN ADDITION TO BEING killed in recreational hunting and for fashion, animals play a major role in other forms of human entertainment. Horses are used in rodeos, bullfights, the steeplechase, recreational riding, pulling carriages for tourists, racing and other equestrian events.

In addition to being kept as pets, dogs are specially bred for kennel shows, obedience contests, fighting, racing, security and protection, and for aiding in the seizure of illegal drugs. Dogs have been used in warfare since ancient times. It is estimated that about 200 Vietnam War dogs survived the war to be assigned to other U.S. bases outside the United States. The remaining dogs were either euthanized or left behind.

Camel and elephant rides are popular attractions at zoos, amusement parks and the circus, while the acrobatics of dolphins, seals and beluga whales are featured at dozens of aquaria around the world.

Animals are also used extensively in advertising, television and the movies. While some are so highly trained that they become film stars (like Lassie, Flipper and Mr. Ed), the majority are used anonymously in action scenes, such as battles and natural disasters. Their participation often involves prolonged captivity, stress, heat exhaustion and even death before the camera, if the scene calls for it.

Because animals have been used in human entertainment for so many years, horseracing, circuses, and dog shows have become traditions (if not cherished institutions) in our society. It is only recently that humans have become sensitized to the idea that such activities involve the animal's forced captivity, degradation, depersonalization, stress and suffering. More and more people are beginning to see that all animals have rights and should not be treated as objects for human pleasure and entertainment.

The subject of animals for entertainment and companionship encompasses a wide range of concerns. In the following pages we'll examine some of the more widespread uses of animals, and will see how a new attitude towards animals is essential if we are to create a just and compassionate world.

Animals for Entertainment

Gambling

Although the origin of gambling is subject to speculation, it is a fact that gambling has involved the exploitation of animals for thousands of years. At the present time, animals play a central role in three major spectator sports which involve gambling: horseracing, dog-racing and to a lesser extent, cock-fighting. Because large amounts of money are staked on the animals' performance, many abuses, such as drugging, biological manipulation and torture, are common.

Dogs

Greyhounds, for example, are gentle by nature but are often trained to become aggressive through systematic starvation. An estimated 90 per cent of greyhound trainers use live lures (such as rabbits) to make the hungry greyhounds race. Animal welfare groups estimate that some 100,000 small animals are torn apart annually during the training and racing of greyhounds. Dogs that are poor racers are often killed or sold to research laboratories. Among racing dogs like the greyhound and whippet, leg and joint fractures are common, and injuries often lead to the animal being destroyed. A similar fate awaits dogs which must be retired after several years of hard racing.

A joint report issued by GREY2K USA and the ASPCA revealed 11,722 Greyhound injuries between 2008 and 2015. More than 3,000 dogs suffered broken legs and other injuries such as crushed skulls, broken backs, paralysis and electrocutions. Such reports- in addition to strong public reaction- has led most U.S. states to ban greyhound racing, although it is still legal in seven states, including Florida. In the decade from 1995 to 2015, the number of greyhounds bred for racing in the United States declined by more than half, and gambling on dog racing fell by two-thirds.

Horses

The use of horses in racing and other equestrian events often involves confinement, stress, injury and other forms of hardship. Horses with broken legs are inevitably destroyed, and many old, sick and feeble animals are sold to slaughterhouses.

Many aspects of horse-racing are rarely seen by the public. In the spring of 1977, for example, the news that a famous jockey was slightly injured made front-page headlines. The fact that three injured horses had to be killed after the race was virtually ignored. A 2016 accident at Gulfsteam Park in Florida involved two horses and three jockeys. One horse – Kandoo- was euthanized after the race and the three jockeys were sent to the hospital, including one with serious internal injuries. When asked to comment on the accident, a jockey who suffered only a sprained ankle said, "I wish that those things never happen, you know they're just animals but it always happens and it's always gonna be happening in this business."

The Circus

How many of us have gone to the circus and watched the horses, lions and elephants perform tricks for our enjoyment? Although the circus has brought pleasure to generations of families, few humans have really observed the circus from the animals' point of view.

Learning tricks goes against the animal's natural instincts, and has been taught under conditions which are demeaning to the animal's innate spirit and pride. During the performance they are subject to ridicule and contempt in order to conform to the image they are supposed to project to the public, such as the "fierce lion", the "funny dog" or the "bungling elephant". After the show, they are imprisoned in tiny cages or trailers, where they spend much of their non-performing hours. Transportation from city to city in cramped conditions subjects the animals to extreme changes in temperature and tremendous physical and psychological wear and tear. When the circus animal is past its prime, it is often sold to a zoo or a roadside animal farm, where lifetime imprisonment and further exploitation usually result.

Rather than merely speak out for more humane conditions for circus animals, many humanitarians have decided to simply avoid patronizing circuses completely while educating the public to any abuses. In addition to reducing the number of people who attend animal-oriented circuses (citing declining attendance, the famous Ringling Bros. and Barnum & Bailey Circus closed in 2017 after 146 years), it has also fueled demand for circus entertainment (such as Circus Vargas, The Imperial Circus, The New Shanghai Circus and the fabulously successful Cirque du Soleil from Québec) that does not use animals in its acts.

Marine Shows

Marine shows and dolphinaria reached their peak of popularity in the 1980s, especially in the United States. It was even believed that dolphinaria would become a major growth industry for at least the rest of the century, and dozens of cities built aquaria as part of their urban renewal programs. Many are now struggling financially.

Those who defend the existence of such aquaria contend that they serve an important educational service and provide a good environment for the study and appreciation of marine life. They also point out that many injured animals are treated in these establishments, and that through contact with humans their own evolution is enhanced.

People who speak out against using dolphins, whales and other marine mammals for research and entertainment while in captivity raise the following ethical points to support their beliefs:

1. Capturing the animals in the ocean is a basic violation of their right to enjoy their lives in a natural habitat;
2. The initial training of these animals often involves deprivation and suffering;
3. The animals suffer when they are transported from one facility to another;
4. Marine animals suffer when they are subjected to changes in temperature and climate;
5. Dolphins and whales are very sensitive to their surroundings and the stress of living in unnatural, cramped quarters increases the chances of disease. A life of boredom, constriction and an early death is guaranteed for captive dolphins and whales.
6. The idea that dolphins and whales benefit from being in the presence of humans is challenged as speciesist and chauvinistic, and not supported by the evidence.

The increase in the commerce of small whales and dolphins has been paralleled by their increasing exploitation by the military. Dolphins are being trained in torpedo recovery, espionage and suicide missions. Much of the original information used in military strategy and operations was taken from early research undertaken at public aquaria. Although the demand for capture and public display of dolphins has been increasing in China, many other countries- including Australia, Chile, Costa Rica, Hungary, Cyprus, Switzerland, Vietnam, Malaysia and Mexico have banned their import, export and /or captive dolphin displays.

It is hoped that our future contact with sea mammals will be based more on respect for their natural way of life than on our desire for personal entertainment. In the words of the celebrated marine conservationist and researcher Jacques-Yves Cousteau:

> Perhaps the time has come to formulate a
> moral code which would govern our relations
> with the great creatures of the sea as well as
> with those on dry land. That this will come to
> pass is our greatest wish. If human
> civilization is going to invade the waters of
> the earth, let it then be first of all to carry a
> message of respect - respect for all life.

Zoos

For over a century, the zoological park has been an almost unquestioned institution in our society. Like the circus, the zoo is primarily a place where animals are kept on display to provide humans with entertainment and a certain degree of education.

If anything, a zoo should serve as a sanctuary when injured or endangered animals have nowhere to go. One of the major accomplishments of certain zoos has been to provide sanctuary to certain endangered species so that they could reproduce without being experimented on for financial gain. Other zoos have undertaken programs in the animals' natural habitats to help preserve their environment and protect them from poachers.

Education has been advanced as a major function of zoos, but many feel that this term is over-used. It is noted that the educational value of captive animals is comparatively small: we observe that an elephant prefers to sleep standing up instead of sleeping on concrete; that lions are rather impatient when kept in a caged enclosure; that captive monkeys are just as obsessed with sex as humans are when living under stress in close quarters.

Although professional zoos have existed for generations, comparatively few valid observations and data have come from them. Growth, reproduction and the habits of captive animals provide the bulk of the information. Most valid observations must be made on animals living normal lives in their natural habitats.

According to David Hancocks of the Woodland Park Zoological Gardens in Seattle:

> The ultimate goal for justifying the existence of a zoo is the creation of an informed, aware and sympathetic public, who will, through the experiences and insights gained from visits to the zoo, be excited about animals to such an extent that they will rouse from their apathy and demand the cessation of the indiscriminate and wasteful destruction of the planet's wildlife and wild habitats.

In actual practice, however, many zoos fall far short of the ideal. According to a 2013 report by Dr. Paul O'Donoghue, a conservation geneticist with the Aspinall Foundation (a British animal conservation society), fewer than one percent of zoo species are part of any serious conservation effort, with many being inbred and having little "genetic integrity" and "no conservation value."

Many other zoos are keeping most of their animals in a state of deprivation that contributes to emotional stress, disease and shorter life spans. A survey of the records of 4,500 elephants both in the wild and in captivity published in *Science* in 2008 found that the median life span for an African elephant in a zoo was 16.9 years, whereas African elephants that lived on a nature preserve died of natural causes at a median age of 56. The researchers concluded that "bringing elephants into zoos profoundly impairs their viability."

For many zoos, their prestige revolves around the number and species they contain. Although hunting and trapping have been largely responsible for the decimation of exotic species during the past century, the demand for these animals by zoos has also taken a major toll in the wild. And although the zoo exists ideally as a final sanctuary for endangered animals, its very existence can encourage the further destruction of the animals' natural habitat, since the animals will supposedly "always have a place to go".

With much of the zoos' attention focused on endangered and exotic species, serious problems develop regarding the welfare of less-desired animals. Since they are raised in a predator-free environment, the zoo often becomes a breeding ground for these animals, and they often become too numerous to maintain. Most surplus animals at a zoo are sold to pet-shops, individuals, or roadside menageries where the animals often suffer tremendous deprivation and hardship. If the animals cannot be sold or given away, they are either used in laboratory experiments or euthanized, their hides sold to tanners and furriers. After a beloved giraffe named Marius was euthanized at Copenhagen Zoo in 2014, EAZA (the European Association of Zoos and Aquaria) revealed that between 3,000 to 5,000 healthy animals are killed in zoos across Europe each year.

Beyond Captivity

Whether zoos are to exist or not, the goal of ahimsa is to place the animal's rights and welfare above human entertainment and profit. Although humane treatment in

175

zoos is important, the long term goal should be to provide every species with an environment which was intended for its natural growth and development. According to author Tom Robbins in his book *Another Roadside Attraction:*

> As unrefined and basic as an animal's emotional equipment maybe, it is not insensitive to freedom. Somewhere in the archives of crudest instinct is recorded the truth that it is better to be endangered and free than captive and comfortable. In the cage, even in the 'environmental parks' which the better zoos are providing for their charges, a creature is out of harmony with the natural rhythms of organ and earth; it must eat foods out of their regular season; soft living erodes its cunning; it becomes confused about mating and often fails to reproduce; an immense *frustration* overtakes it due to an inability to heed instinctual instructions. Were it capable of choice, surely it would prefer to take its chances 'out there' against the odds of hunger and hungry. While suffering is no more glamorous - or even necessary - for animal than for man, and while for the being who is at peace with itself survival may be of trivial concern, still there is something kind of noble in the struggle for survival. Whether meaningful or meaningless, the game of life is there to be played - and the animal in his animal way seems to 'know' it and the cage is an offense to what his inner animal voice tells him is right and true.

Companion Animals

In addition to the ownership of animals by cattle-ranchers, chicken-farmers and mink-breeders, most people can claim to have "owned" a pet at some time during their lives. Although many people have been responsible pet-owners, the concept of a dog or cat as personal property has been responsible for much animal suffering. Because animals are said to exist primarily for our pleasure, they have often become an object of human violence, vanity and neglect.

Respect for animals has been an essential aspect of the teachings of ahimsa since the times of Lord Mahavira. According to the *Śānti parva* or "Book of Peace" of the Hindu epic *Mahabharata,* our highest duty is to secure happiness *(sukha)* for all creatures, especially those who are classified as "mobile". These teachings have helped lay the groundwork for a more enlightened view of companion animals as living, evolving beings in their own right and worthy of our respect, care and protection.

This view of animals can lead us to see ourselves more as their guardians than their owners. Rather than viewing our relationship with them as training them to do our bidding, we can seek to learn from them as well. Their loyalty, their ability to give unconditional affection, and their intuitive approach to life can teach us how to re-connect to our own instinctual nature and to be more centered in our feelings rather than in our mind.

For many people, the companionship of a dog or a cat is essential for their wellbeing. Companion animals have been scientifically proven to help us to reduce stress, have healthier hearts, connect better socially with other people, improve mood and experience greater meaning in life. When grounded in respect and caring, the relationships formed between humans and companion animals can be one of the most rewarding of experiences for everyone involved.

However, at the present time, there are serious problems concerning domestic animals which call for the attention of not just students of ahimsa, but for everyone interested in the welfare of animals.

Perhaps the most serious result of the domestication of animals has been their uncontrolled birthrate. Since most domestic animals are raised in a protected environment, their numbers increase at such a phenomenal rate that there aren't enough homes for them. Only about ten percent of cats and dogs received by animal shelters are spayed or neutered.

In the United States alone, some 2000-3500 dogs and cats are said to be born every *hour*. The following table illustrates how animal overpopulation occurs by counting the total unspayed progeny of an unspayed female dog during a seven-year period:

Year 1.	4 puppies, 2 female	4 animals
Year 2.	1st and 2nd generation of females	
	12 puppies, 6 female	12 animals
Year 3.	3rd generation of females	
	36 puppies, 18 female	36 animals
Year 4.	4th generation of females	
	108 puppies, 54 female	108 animals
Year 5.	5th generation of females	
	324 puppies, 162 female	324 animals
Year 6.	6th generation of females	
	972 puppies, 486 female	972 animals

Year 7.   7th generation of females

2916 puppies, 1458 female   2916 animals

Total Progeny   4372 animals

The fate of unwanted animals is especially serious because they are forced to endure tremendous suffering and deprivation. More often than not, unwanted dogs and cats are abused by their owners. According to the ASPCA, approximately 7.6 million companion animals enter animal shelters in the United States every year. Of those, approximately 3.9 million are dogs and 3.4 million are cats. Of this number, over 2.7 million are destroyed every year, including 1.4 million dogs and 1.3 million cats.

Thousands more are sold to laboratories, where they spend the rest of their lives in the hands of vivisectionists. Countless others are left to fend for themselves, and if they are not killed by cars, people or disease, they continue to reproduce. While figures on the number of stray dogs in the United States are impossible to come by, estimates of the stray cat population alone have been as high as 70 million.

Since humans originated the practice of domesticating animals, their welfare is a human responsibility. In the light of the present overpopulation of these animals and the suffering it involves, their welfare demands our wholehearted attention. The present lack of concern and involvement by members of the community often leaves the responsibility of their care to animal pounds, which are often inadequately funded, overcrowded and poorly managed.

Although there is controversy surrounding the right of humans to control the reproduction process of another species (which - as animal breeders - we have been doing anyway) the enormous number of unwanted pets demands that something be done. The most promising method includes free or low-cost spaying and neutering. While not ahimsic in the strictest sense of the word, these forms of population control have been proven to reduce animal suffering in future generations and are the least violent methods we have at this time. The development of oral contraceptives is perhaps a less himsic alternative to spaying and neutering in the future.

In addition to birth-control, higher license fees for unspayed females and unaltered males, more public participation and support for local animal shelters, and better education regarding responsible pet-care are primary ways to reduce the suffering of companion animals.

Some people would add the adoption of fast and painless methods of euthanasia to help control the overpopulation of unwanted animals. For advocates of ahimsa, however, this may be a difficult idea to accept; putting animals to death simply because they are unwanted may seem unethical, perhaps even comparable to the killing of Jews in Nazi concentration camps during the Holocaust.

Henry Beston, the American writer and naturalist, wrote that perhaps we need a wiser and more mystical concept of animals. Rather than view ourselves as the superior species with the power to dominate over the lives of others, we need to see *Homo sapiens* as a part of the animal kingdom made up of many different "animal nations". When grounded in humility and respect, our relationship with other animal species can be transformed.

Their innate need for freedom can be respected, and their right to a complete life-cycle free of human interference can be guaranteed. By studying other animals in their natural habitats, we not only learn about them as they really are but we come into contact with our human traits of compassion and respect which we need to develop.

And by deepening our connection with the animals in this way, we become more open to their innate wisdom, their beauty, and their zest for living. We begin moving towards achieving a true planetary consciousness, an essential step towards preserving all of the Earth's children.

Part IV

Ahimsa:
A New Ecological Ethic

WITHIN THE PAST FEW DECADES, increasing air, water and land pollution has brought the issue of ecology - the study of the relationship between living beings and their environment - into sharp focus. Although much has been written about ecology (the term itself has become a household word) only a small percentage of us really take it seriously.

Few people realize, for example, that ecology contains a concept which is as revolutionary as anything since Copernicus discovered that the Earth was not the centre of the universe. Instead of the long-accepted teachings that assume the exclusive dignity of humans and their independent superiority, dominion and license to subjugate the Earth, ecology teaches simply that human beings are *not* the centre of life on this planet. It stresses that not only are we tied to nature, but we are a *part* of nature.

Through the study of ecology, science has begun to understand the great systems of order which underlie and guide the complex flow of life on this planet. To the surprise of many investigators, this quest has taken us far beyond the realm of scientific thought and into deep mystical understanding. Like religion, ecology seeks to reveal the ancient mysteries of life itself, and can help us chart a course of evolution which will ensure a future for all of us who live on the Earth. By making use of the tools of logic, deduction, intuition and analysis, ecology may prove to be the first true science/religion. Theologian and philosopher Albert Schweitzer wrote movingly of this possibility many years ago:

> The deeper we look into nature, the more we
> recognize that it is full of life, and the more
> profoundly we know that all life is a secret
> and that we are united with all life in nature.
> Man can no longer live his life for himself

alone. We realize that all life is valuable and
that we are united to all this life. From this
knowledge comes our spiritual relationship to
the universe.

One of the basic laws of ecology teaches that every
living thing has a reason for being here, a mission to
accomplish, and has been given a special function in the
scheme of things. The earliest teachings of ahimsa - like
those of modern ecology - have taught that the entire
planet is *one body* and that every living thing is part of the
whole.

If this "body" is to survive, we must learn to respect
it as we must learn to respect ourselves, and as we seek to
love ourselves, we must also seek to love and respect all
forms of life which share this planetary system with us. In
his book, *The Ecological Conscience,* Robert Bisch wrote
about the need to develop an ecological conscience which

> . . . must teach man that there is no natural
> right to exterminate a form of life; that one is
> not entitled to desecrate the earth, air, water
> or space merely because he happens to own,
> control, or occupy some portion of it; and the
> fact of 'legality' in a human court cannot
> remove ecological crimes from having
> planetary implications.

Ahimsa teaches that all life is interrelated and
interdependent, and that each living thing depends on
another for ensuring its survival. Grass, for example,
provides nourishment for millions of tiny invertebrates,
which in turn are food for insects. The insects are eaten by
frogs and small birds, which provide nourishment for
larger animals. When the larger animals die, they provide
food for other living things, and when they die and

decompose, they fertilize the soil on which grass is grown. If this food chain is disrupted, the very fiber of life on this planet is affected. As with a house of cards, the removal of one card brings about the collapse of the entire structure.

During the past several hundred years (and the past fifty years in particular), humans have been destroying the planet at an accelerated pace. We have polluted the water, poisoned the air, and disfigured the land. We have upset many of the natural biological processes that are essential to the continued well-being of life on this planet. The action of humans against the planet has been leading to the destruction of the *biosphere,* the fragile envelope of our planet which contains life.

The biosphere is a mixture of oxygen, nitrogen, carbon dioxide, argon gas, water vapor and other elements, and is produced by the plants, animals and earth-borne bacteria that use these elements and return them in the same measure. This continuous cycle of give-and-take creates the balance by which all life is maintained.

As a living and evolving being, the Earth's natural survival mechanisms have only one object; to preserve the conditions that permit life to exist and flourish. The steadiness of much of the planet's surface temperature at 60-100 degrees Fahrenheit, the regulation of the amount of salt (3.4 per cent) in the oceans, the stabilization of the oxygen concentration of the atmosphere (at 21 per cent), the controlled presence of a small amount of ammonia in the atmosphere, and the existence of the now-threatened ozone layer in the upper atmosphere to protect plants and animals from harmful ultra-violet rays all reveal the goal to protect, nurture and sustain life. Any significant changes in this balance would lead to extinction of life as we know it.

Global Warming- defined as "the increase of Earth's average surface temperature due to effect of greenhouse gases, such as carbon dioxide emissions from burning fossil fuels or from deforestation, which trap heat that would otherwise escape from Earth," is now accepted as scientific fact.

Photographs of the Earth from outer space have shown it to be not unlike a beautiful blue pearl that encompasses all planetary life in oneness. In the words of the late Ambassador Adlai E. Stevenson:

> We travel together, passengers on a little
> spaceship, dependent on its vulnerable
> resources of air and soil; all committed for
> our safety and security and peace; preserved
> from annihilation only by the care, the work,
> and I will say, the love we give our fragile
> craft.

As the nurturing mother to all of us, the continued ability of the Earth to survive is largely dependent on what we - Her children - can do to nurture and protect our planetary home.

Chapter 11

Ahimsa towards the Earth:
An Alternative to Terracide

To issue from the workshops of Nature,
a thing must be worthy of Nature's loving care
and most painstaking art.
Should it not be worthy of your respect at least?

-Mikhail Naimy

THE EARTH IS A LIVING body pulsating with energy. Even during a short walk in the forest, we can see that it is teeming with life. Mosses, shrubs, flowers and trees of different sizes are all around us, full of variety and beauty. Birds are calling to each other, squirrels, chipmunks and other animals are scurrying about, and insects seem to be flying everywhere, each on a seemingly important mission. If we are lucky, we will see a deer or other large animal. During our walk, perhaps we will cross a rushing stream or stand near a crashing waterfall. Or we may sit quietly within a grove of trees, as the breeze gently moves through the branches and leaves.

At once, nature seems extremely alive and powerful as the sole supporter of all these life forms. We feel the vastness, the quiet strength, and the generosity of the Earth towards all of its creations. We feel secure in these natural surroundings, and acknowledge our kinship with the other life forms which share this planet with us.

Of all the issues which confront humanity, there is no greater concern than the survival of the planet itself. As a great living body that provides food, shelter and sustenance, the Earth is essentially - as Native Americans have taught - our "Mother" in the deepest and most inclusive sense of the word. In spite of Her vastness, strength and generosity, the planet is being abused by humans at an unceasing rate. Since we are totally dependent on the Earth's life support systems for our own survival and well-being, Her health and survival are of paramount concern to all of us. Terracide, defined as "the destruction of a planet or of natural ecosystems" is happening every single day.

Despite the fact that Earth Day began in 1970, more substantial changes need to take place on a global scale regarding environmental pollution, global warming, the proper use and conservation of what we like to call "our" natural resources, and the widespread reliance on fossil fuels and nuclear energy.

Ecologists point out that although a growing awareness of environmental issues is important, too many of us are committed to the *idea* of ecology rather than its *substance.* They warn that if we expect the planet to survive, we need to make a far greater personal commitment to protecting the environment than we have in the past. Any act of protection - whether collecting plastic bottles for recycling or participating in a demonstration to close a nuclear dump - is good and useful. But when performed as part of one's commitment to ahimsa, every outward act takes on a deeper, more inclusive significance. It reflects our decision to harm no one and to save the Earth from injury and destruction.

The critical situation calls upon each member of the human species to become - to the best of one's ability - an *earthsteward*: an enlightened, compassionate and nurturing human being who is dedicated to protecting and preserving Mother Earth.

The work of an earthsteward - a true soldier of ahimsa - is not to be taken lightly. The sacred task of defending and protecting the Earth is as serious as protecting one's own human mother if a potential murderer or rapist were to attack her at home or in the street.

As many of us are aware, there are presently a multitude of threats to the survival of this planet. Nuclear war aside, they tend to focus primarily on four major areas of concern:

Land Erosion

According to the Food and Agricultural Organization of the United Nations (FAO), over 2 billion hectares (5 billion acres) of topsoil are lost each year: an annual loss of an estimated 25 billion tons of soil from croplands alone in excess of new soil formation. China's Huang (Yellow) River alone dumps 1600 million tons of soil a year into the sea. The United States has lost about one-third of its topsoil since settled agriculture began. The FAO warns that worldwide, soil erosion puts the livelihoods of nearly 1 billion people at risk.

The erosion of cropland is largely due to modern intensive farming methods, the utilization of heavy farm equipment, the use of chemical pesticides and fertilizers, the destruction of green belts on farms in order to have more land for cash crops, and the practice of not leaving cropland fallow. Letting the land "rest" for a season or more enhances the natural ability of the soil to restore its depleted nutrients.

Loss of topsoil has also come about through the unrestricted and poorly planned growth of cities and suburbs. The construction of new highways, industrial plants, shopping centers and tract housing have destroyed vast areas of green space that prevented soil erosion and maintained the stability of the local ecosystem for thousands of years.

The Protection of Forests

Closely related to soil erosion is the widespread destruction of forests. Human expansion into forested areas due to road construction, cattle ranching and housing development has decimated forests all over the planet. The increased consumption of wood for houses, furniture, packaging, newsprint and other paper products has also taken a major toll. Not only has it reduced the Earth's topsoil layer through erosion, but it has also helped eliminate a primary source of oxygen that is vital for the survival of humans and other animal species.

In the Amazon River basin, the destruction of the forest has been especially intense. Rainforests are the most biologically diverse region on Earth, and contain over 40 per cent of all the animal and plant species identified by scientists. At the present time, five to ten species a day are being exterminated through forest destruction, including species of plants which may hold vital medicinal properties for human health. Much of this destruction involves short term profits for speculators. In addition to exotic hardwoods like mahogany, Palo Santo and rosewood, soft trees for paper pulp are also being cut: the United States alone imports some more than $210 million worth of paper from Brazil each year, much of it from rainforests.

Millions of acres of tropical forests - especially in Central and South America - are also lost through their conversion into grasslands for cattle production (much of which ends up as meat in fast food restaurants and pet food in North American and European industrialized nations). In some countries, such as India and Nepal, many of the remaining forests are being stripped for fuel in heating and cooking, as the local people who are poor and hungry will often destroy their immediate environment in order to ensure their short-term survival. All in all, the rate of destruction of forests - at the rate of 95 acres per *minute* - is far greater than the rate of replanting them. When forests and other green areas disappear, a situation is created which holds extremely serious consequences for the planet's survival. St. Barbe Baker, the renowned "Man of the Trees" addressed this issue back in 1985:

> Of the Earth's 30 billion acres, already 9
> billion are desert. We look at it this way:
> plastic surgeons tell us that if a man loses
> one-third of his skin, he dies: he has 'had it'.
> As a botanist and arboriculturist, I know that
> if a tree loses one-third of its bark it dies. I,
> therefore, submit that if Earth loses one-third
> of its green mantle of trees and other healthy
> vegetation, it, too, will die - the water table
> will sink beyond recall, and life on this planet
> will become impossible.

Recycle!

Recycling has been an environmental goal for several decades, and when practiced, has provided major and multiple benefits to both humanity and the Earth as a whole. According to the United Nations Food and

Agriculture Organization (FAO), 397.6 million tons of paper and paperboard were produced worldwide in 2013. Most of the paper produced today (54 percent in 2013) is used for wrapping and packaging purposes, followed by printing and writing (26 percent), newsprint (7 percent), and household and sanitary tissues (8 percent).

According to the Worldwatch Institute, paper recycling helps to reduce energy use and pollution. On average, paper fibers can be recycled five to seven times before they become unusable. Recycled paper requires 60 percent less energy and 80 percent less water to produce than virgin paper, and it generates 95 percent less air pollution. Recycling one ton of paper on average saves 7,000 gallons (26,500 liters) of water, about 84 gallons (318 liters) of oil, and 4,100 kilowatt-hours of electricity. According to the University of Colorado's Environmental Center, one ton of recycled paper (909 kilograms) saves 3,700 pounds (1,682 kilograms) of lumber and 24,000 gallons (90,849 liters) of water; it also uses 64 percent less energy and 50 percent less water to produce. It also creates 74 percent less air pollution, saves 17 trees, and even creates five times more jobs than one ton of paper products from virgin wood pulp.

Recycling paper, iron and steel not only substantially reduces the use of energy, but reduces the amount of solid waste and air pollution involved in paper, iron and steel production as well. The recycling of aluminum cans alone reduces air pollution by 95 per cent over taking aluminum from the land directly and processing it in a smelter.

Recycling computers, printers and other office machines- along with other types of electronics- is another way to help protect the environment. No fewer than 17 different metals can be recycled from a cell phone alone, including 0.008 grams of gold, 0.07 grams of silver and 0.006 grams of palladium, along with a number of lanthanides or "rare earth" elements like neodymium and dysprosium.

A growing number of retailers that sell office technology and other electronics receive computers, video equipment, printers, televisions other electronics for recycling from the public. Customers can bring any brand of office equipment or electronics in any condition, regardless of where it was purchased, and it is recycled at no cost. Many cities offer electronics recycling programs as well. By 2015, some 26.5 million pounds of electronics were recycled worldwide, with a goal of 40 million pounds by 2020. Many office supply stores recycle empty printer ink cartridges. Over 56.8 million such cartridges were recycled worldwide by one large American retailer in a recent year.

There is also an increasing demand for recycling furniture. For example, Davies Office, located in upstate New York, has become a leading provider of high-quality remanufactured office furniture that has been transformed to look and perform like new. Their inventory includes refurbished office cubicles, workstations, desks, tables, chairs, and credenzas at a fraction of the cost of new office furniture. And environmentally-conscious shoppers can often find excellent deals on used household furniture at thrift shops, yard sales and online.

While the amount of recycling has increased over the past few decades, there is still much to be done. When compared to other countries, the United States ranks seventh in the world. Switzerland- which ranks number 1- recycles nearly twice as much waste per capita as the U.S.A. One of the most positive trends has been the increased recycling of aluminum cans. In the United States, the rate was barely 17 percent in 1972, but by 2013, it reached 66.7 percent. The recycling rate of plastic containers in the U.S.A. still lags that of aluminum cans: although it reached over 30 percent by 2013- representing 2.9 billion pounds- a modest 0.4 percent over the previous year.

Reducing Food Waste

According to the United States Environmental Protection Agency (EPA) over 33 million tons of food was thrown into landfills in a recent year. This is equal to one pound of food per person per day. In addition to Americans' insistence on buying only "perfect" fruits and vegetables, approximately 25 percent of the food Americans buy is thrown out every year due to buying unneeded food, over-preparation (i.e., making too much food for a meal) as well as poor storage and subsequent spoilage.

Food not eaten in restaurants can be taken home and eaten later, and restaurants can donate excess food to food banks and other charities. Fruits and vegetables that may have bruises or other imperfections are often perfectly good to eat and should not be thrown away. Supermarkets can offer "imperfect" food to customers at a discount. Instead of throwing imperfect food and not-so-fresh food away, they can donate it to local hunger relief organizations.

In England, food waste campaigners from the Real Junk Food Project have begun opening "warehouse" stores that sell food discarded from supermarkets and other food-related businesses. The food is sold on a "pay as you feel" basis and feeds thousands of families a week. A similar project (WeFood) was started in Denmark by Folkekirkens Nødhjælp, a charity that had opened two stores by early 2017. Every year more than 700,000 tons of food are wasted in Denmark. After being open just six months, WeFood received over 40 tons of food that would have otherwise been destroyed. The project is part of a government initiative to reduce food waste.

In addition to buying only what we actually plan to eat (and eating what we have bought at the market before we buy more) creative cooks can learn how to use what is often thrown away. For example, beet tops can be cooked and eaten like collard greens; broccoli stalks can be grated, frozen, and used later as an ingredient in soup. Other food can go into compost rather than landfills.

Protecting the Earth from Pollution

The threat of destruction of the biosphere from water, air and solid waste pollution is perhaps humanity's greatest challenge. The death of lakes from acid rain has already been documented, while the pollution of lakes, rivers and oceans from human sewage, animal feedlots and industrial waste has received extensive attention in the media. The destruction of forests by acid rain resulting from industrial pollution and motor vehicle exhaust continues to require immediate action, especially in China and India, among the highest emitters of sulfur dioxide in the world.

In addition to causing acid rain, air pollution from factories and motor vehicles has been a primary cause of the destruction of the ozone layer in the upper atmosphere. The loss of this protective shield from the sun's ultraviolet rays has been linked to depressed immune levels and cancer among humans and other animals. Increased levels of carbon dioxide in the atmosphere from car exhaust can alter weather patterns and increase the surface temperature of the Earth, which threatens to melt the polar ice caps. This melting can raise the sea-level, profoundly affecting those who reside in the coastal areas of the world.

In addition to autos and trucks, major polluters include jet aircraft, power plants, refuse dumps and incinerators, pulp and paper mills, iron and steel mills, oil refineries, smelters and chemical plants. When measured on a per-capita basis, the annual air pollution figures of the average person living in the United States is as follows:

Climate Change Pollution (CO_2) = 27 tons
Ozone-Causing Pollution (NOx) = 102 pounds
Acid Rain Causing Pollution (SO_2) = 129 pounds
Small Particulate Pollution = 14 pounds
Toxic Lead Pollution (Pb) = 0.4 ounces
Toxic Mercury Pollution (Hg) = 0.01 ounces

A 2016 World Health Organization (WHO) air quality model confirms that 92 percent of the world's population lives in places where air quality levels exceed WHO limits. According to its 2016 report *Ambient air pollution: A global assessment of exposure and burden of disease*, there was an 8 percent increase in air pollution between 2008 and 2013, primarily in the Eastern Mediterranean, South Asia, East Asia and the Western Pacific regions of the world. China and India are considered the most polluted countries on Earth, and they led the world in both the number of deaths and deaths per capita attributed to ambient air pollution.

Water pollution is believed to be the leading worldwide cause of deaths and diseases, and that it accounts for the deaths of more than 14,000 people a day. In the United States alone, some 44 percent of stream miles, 64 percent of lake acres, and 30 percent of bays and estuaries were classified as polluted in a recent year. The drinking water of 90 percent of Chinese cities is considered polluted, and by 2007, one quarter the length of China's seven main rivers were so poisoned that the water harmed the skin. The biggest contributors to water pollution around the world include pathogens from human and farm animal waste, storm drains, detergents, insecticides and herbicides, and industrial discharge, including chemical solvents.

Like the very real threat of nuclear war, the possibility that our planetary home will die from pollution, abuse and neglect seems almost too terrible to contemplate. For this reason, the challenges involved in saving the Earth's life support systems seem nothing short of overwhelming. One cannot help experiencing tremendous sadness and despair when confronted with the possibility of the extinction of life on Earth.

We can deal with this threat in several ways. Like the people who prefer simply to "cut off" from their feelings about nuclear war, the vast majority of humanity chooses not to take the ecological destruction of the planet to heart. As a result of this psychic numbing, one's individual integrity is severely compromised and personal power is given away to the very individuals (such as politicians, industrialists and other decision-makers) who are actively involved in the systematic destruction of our planetary home.

An Ahimsic Paradigm

Ahimsa towards the Earth is our only alternative to terracide. When confronted with destruction on such a broad and intensified scale, the ahimsic goals of respect, harmlessness and creative action can overcome passivity and resignation. A true soldier of ahimsa is a spiritual warrior who will not stand around and do nothing when violence or any other form of himsa is being perpetrated on another life form, be it a neighbor, a dog, a tree, or a lake or stream. For this reason, the doctrine of ahimsa is the very essence of the science of ecology, and calls on every single individual to do whatever is in his or her personal power to help save the planet from destruction.

The call for planetary stewardship requires both a deep sensitivity towards the Earth and a strong commitment to action. Awareness towards even the smallest (and to our eyes) even the least significant form of life was stressed by the earliest teachers of ahimsa, the

197

Jains. According to an early Jain sutra, a religious person was forbidden to dig into the ground without good reason, and was advised not to uproot trees, trample on lawns, pluck leaves or flowers and immature fruits from trees. A good contemporary application was shared by Rick Day, who lived and worked at a spiritual community in upstate New York:

> The combined efforts of our contractor, the maintenance staff, and volunteers resulted in the completion of the installation of the Hill House septic system. We installed it without damaging the environment. We took up the grassy sod before digging. The tree limbs were tied out of the way. Ditches were dug by hand so as not to damage the large tree roots. After-ward the sod was replaced and bare areas seeded. I like this new way of working in harmony with surrounding life. It is a manifestation of all our love.

Nevertheless, realism shows us that in order for one form of life to exist, other life forms are destroyed. And although other living beings are bound to be killed in order to ensure our survival (even with every breath we take, we are killing millions of tiny microbes) teachers of ahimsa, like Albert Schweitzer, point to the importance of doing the *least harm possible* to other living things:

> Whenever I injure life of any sort, I must be quite clear whether it is necessary. Beyond the unavoidable, I must never go, not even with what seems insignificant. The farmer, who has mown down a thousand flowers in his meadow as fodder for his cows, must be careful on his way home not to strike off in

wanton pastime the head of a single flower by
the roadside, for he thereby commits a wrong
against life without being under the pressure
of necessity.

As evidenced by the life of Albert Schweitzer, one of
the primary steps towards the realization of ahimsa
towards the Earth is opening our hearts completely to
nature. As Native American elders have taught, only by
developing a close, intimate relationship with the Earth
Mother and Her children can we fully participate in Her
protection and care. "Walking in balance on the Earth
Mother" with an attitude of humility and reverence has
been the essential teaching of native peoples throughout
the world for thousands of years.

Respect for the land, the trees, the mountains,
streams and lakes not only helped ensure the survival of
native peoples, but helped them develop a powerful and
even mystical relationship with the land and its
inhabitants. Unfortunately, many of these early traditions
of respect and planetary stewardship have become lost as
native peoples have been assimilated into modern
industrial society. However, the keepers of these early
ahimsic traditions have become increasingly heard as we
seek to understand the knowledge and wisdom inherent in
their lost way of life.

Practical Ahimsic Strategies

How can this intimate relationship come about? Some may
be called to spend many days, months or even years in a
more natural environment, quietly learning the ways of the
Earth and understanding its rhythms.

Others will grow houseplants, begin a garden, or
plant trees to learn about the mysteries of growth and
transformation. Some will choose a path involving study,

observation and quiet contemplation, while others will prefer more dynamic activities like whitewater rafting, mountain climbing, skiing, hiking or scuba diving.

Still others may choose to deepen their understanding of nature by taking part in ancient native rituals and ceremonies which honor the Earth environment and open us to Earth wisdom. The classic vision quest of the Native Americans - where an individual spends several days and nights alone in nature to obtain guidance - has been seen as a powerful method for understanding our true relationship to the Earth and in finding our task in life which will aid in Her protection.

Another sacred path used to attain Earth wisdom is through exploring our relationships with trees, waterfalls, lakes, mountaintops and other "power spots" in nature. Grounding ourselves in nature and being open to earth teachings enables us to achieve greater inner harmony and self-healing. Taking photographs of a waterfall, or sitting quietly while sketching a mountain or a flower can intensify our powers of observation and deepen our appreciation of the beauty around us.

For urban dwellers, the appreciation of nature can take place in one's own neighborhood. Adopting a tree (or several) on one's street, watering it, and keeping it free of debris can benefit the natural urban environment. Walking through a local park with a large garbage bag and filling it with discarded bottles, cans, papers and other rubbish can be one of the most satisfying ecological activities for a city resident. Getting involved with (or founding) a local "friends of the park" organization, planting trees, starting an urban garden, creating "vest pocket" parks in vacant lots can all express our feelings of love and respect for the Earth in a practical and lasting way.

Exploring Personal Earthiness

Yet another essential aspect to our understanding nature is to get in touch with our own earthiness: the instinctual, intuitive and natural side of our beings. As we have become accustomed to air conditioning, shopping malls, artificial environments and electronic gadgetry, we have also moved away from our former status as natural beings who were once in touch with the rhythms of the Earth and who lived on the land with an attitude of reverence and respect.

Learning how to be "grounded" in nature and to become more comfortable with our instinctual side can be a very exciting experience. Becoming acquainted with and participating in traditional ceremonies of early native peoples can help us forge a sense of participation with the forces of nature that can eventually transform our everyday lives. By consciously seeking to contact and resonate with the subtle energies of nature found in lakes, caves, trees, waterfalls and oceans, we can intensify our awareness, self-healing and self-transformation.

We can also increase our appreciation of our own earthiness by getting into greater contact with our body and our emotions. Learning to appreciate and accept our bodies is often difficult, as many of us have been conditioned over the years to believe that the human body is ugly, that its feelings are not to be trusted and by following our basic instincts we will get ourselves (and others) into trouble.

However, by exploring our images, experiences and feelings with ourselves and others, we can begin to discard such images and reclaim our bodies and become more sensitive to their genuine needs. As we gradually become more connected to our body, we can begin to treat it with more care and respect. Because each of us is but a cell in the body of humanity, caring for one's own body in this way is an important first step in caring for the body of humanity - and the entire planet - as a whole.

Earth's Ten Commandments

From a color poster by David Lance Goines, 1990
Text by Ernest "Chick" Callenbach

Chapter 12

Ahimsa and Energy

We are the curators of life on Earth. We hold it in the palm of our hand. We're at the crossroads of time, right now. . . . If we don't get rid of nuclear power and nuclear weapons, we won't survive. Neither will the animals and plants.

-Dr. Helen Caldicott

ENERGY PERMEATES THE ENTIRE universe. Energies and forces are pouring upon our planet potently and ceaselessly, and have been behind the cycle of creation since the beginning of time. Energy permeates everything in nature and animates all life on Earth.

Human beings have a unique role regarding energy. In addition to learning how to channel our own personal energy (manifested in our thoughts, emotions and deeds), we also have the responsibility to channel and utilize planetary forces and energy to aid the evolution of all life. Because energy is a resource that can be used in both benign and malevolent ways, we need to understand its power and learn how to channel it in safe directions which do not bring harm to the planet or its citizens. On the following pages, we'll briefly examine some of the issues surrounding energy and ahimsa, and explore both existing energy sources as well as emerging energy technologies that can enhance the quality of life of all the Earth's inhabitants.

In addition to the primary direct energy we receive from the Sun, energy is indirectly obtained from plants, from moving air (wind) and from the moving water in rivers and ocean tides. Energy can be produced through the combustion of certain materials like coal or oil, by the interaction of one substance with another (such as the reaction of solar photovoltaic cells with solar radiation), or by the breaking down of elements as seen in nuclear fission. Some forms of energy, such as solar, are in unlimited supply, while others, including coal, oil, water or uranium are available in limited amounts or are not equally distributed through the planet for general use.

At the present time, the global consumption of energy is increasing dramatically each year, especially in the developing nations of the world. Bearing in mind that some 70 per cent of the world's population resides in these nations, their need for energy is expected to increase sharply by the end of the century. This demand will be all the more acute since many of those living in the developing nations of the world demand a standard of living which resembles that presently enjoyed by those living in developed industrialized nations like the United States, Canada, Britain and Japan.

For a student of ahimsa, the subject of energy is fundamental, because it is closely linked to all aspects of reverence for life. Whether we are speaking of the economic hardship imposed on consumers forced to pay for expensive energy, the environmental damage a power plant can bring to a forest, or the political conflicts that result from the fight to obtain finite energy resources, the need for an ahimsic approach to a global energy policy is important for our time.

There are presently several available paths which will help us move towards both a personal and global energy policy based on respect for the Earth Mother and "all our relatives". They include conserving the energy already available to us, as well as the development and utilization of energy technologies which do not pose a threat to life on Earth.

Conservation

Conservation of the energy we presently use is an important aspect of an ahimsic energy policy. Not only does it lessen our dependency on prevailing energy sources like coal, oil and nuclear energy that pose a threat to the environment and human health, energy conservation reduces the demand for additional power plants in the future. For example, the reduction in the demand for energy in the United States during the 1970s played a major role in cancelling plans to build eighty-seven nuclear power plants between 1975 and 1984. Even in a country like the United Kingdom, the European Group for Ecological Action (Ecoropa) estimated that conservation can reduce energy consumption there by 27 per cent.

Since the early 1970s, the energy efficiency of factories and public buildings has increased tremendously. Programs to insulate and weatherproof homes, commercial buildings and schools were established as energy (especially oil) became more expensive than in previous years. The recycling of paper, iron and steel and aluminum brought energy benefits as well, because it takes far less energy to recycle these resources than to produce them from raw materials. According to the Worldwatch Institute, the reduction of energy to produce recycled paper over "new" paper ranges from 30 to 55 per cent, while the corresponding figures for aluminum are 90-95 per cent and 60-70 per cent for recycling iron and steel.

Unfortunately, many aspects of our consumer-orientated society continue to require vast amounts of energy. Many of the products we purchase are energy-intensive in their manufacture, require energy for their use, and are built so that the item costs more to repair than replace. Consumer demand for quality products that can be easily repaired will reduce this trend towards disposable goods, which are harmful to the environment as garbage in addition to being wasteful of energy in their manufacture.

In addition, the use of non-electric coffee-makers, mixers, and other household appliances will not only make for a simpler lifestyle, but will save energy in their use. Where electrical appliances are needed, more attention can be given to their energy efficiency than to style or color. In addition, such appliances can be used only when necessary in order to reduce overall energy consumption in the home. By paying attention to the little things, much can be done to help reduce energy consumption in the home.

There are plenty of ways to save energy that take very little effort and can reduce household energy consumption by 20 percent or more. Here are twelve general suggestions offered by Silicon Valley Power in Santa Clara, California, with more details available on its website (http://www.siliconvalleypower.com):

1. When you're at home, keep thermostats set for energy economy
2. When you go to sleep, set thermostats for low energy use

3. When you go out, set your thermostats for low energy use
4. If a room is not in use, don't heat or cool it more than necessary
5. Adjust heating and cooling systems to work more efficiently
6. Cool your home the natural way (using open windows and fans)
7. Let the sun help heat your home in cold weather
8. "Button up" your home to retain cool or heated air
9. Keep your body comfortably warm or cool
10. Use less hot water in the bathroom, kitchen, and laundry
11. Use your lights, TV, and other appliances wisely
12. Buy more energy-efficient light bulbs

Packaging

The packaging we use for the products we buy also requires large amounts of energy. In addition to the chemicals, wood and plastics needed to produce boxes, padding, bags and wrapping paper, the environmental cost for their disposal is extremely high. According to the United States Environmental Protection Agency, over 360 *billion* BTUs of energy could have been saved if the 1986 per capita packaging consumption had remained at the per capita levels of 1958. This saving could have amounted to more than 267,000 barrels of oil per day - more than a 42 per cent saving over the energy currently being used for packaging nationwide.

In addition to the conscious recycling of packaging materials, including plastic bags used to pack various foods, bringing one's own bag or knapsack to the supermarket is an excellent way to save plastic and paper bags at the checkout counter. By speaking out against the use of elaborate packaging materials to both merchants and manufacturers, one can lobby for the reduction and elimination of unnecessary boxes and bags. In addition to saving energy and trees, the environmental problems caused by their disposal are substantially reduced.

Transportation

After the 1972-73 Arab oil embargo, the family car has changed dramatically. Between 1975 and 1983, for example, the average weight for cars manufactured in the United States decreased by 26 per cent, while the average fuel economy increased by nearly 60 per cent. Although this trend produced many positive results concerning both reduced energy consumption and less environmental pollution, various oil price slumps over the years have brought about an increased demand for larger, less fuel-efficient cars. This phenomenon showed that people rely more on economic factors to determine their buying habits than concerns about energy conservation or the environment.

For those interested in saving energy and setting an example for their neighbors, smaller energy-efficient vehicles-including hybrid and electric- are a must, and even these should be used only when necessary. Alternative transportation can also be considered. Among all types of urban transportation, a bicycle is by far the most energy-efficient, utilizing 50 per cent less energy (200 BTUs per passenger mile) than even walking. Walking is an estimated ten times more energy-efficient than taking a bus, while a car is the least efficient method, using over 12,000 BTUs for every passenger-mile with two people sharing the car. For inter-urban transportation, a loaded bus is by far the most energy-efficient method of transport, followed by the train, car and airplane.

Eating Lower on the Food Chain

Another way to conserve energy is through our eating habits. In addition to choosing foods that involve a minimum of commercial processing and packaging, a shift from animal protein towards the direct consumption of plant protein can not only lower cholesterol levels in the body, but can generate substantial energy savings worldwide.

When we consider the actual calories of energy needed to produce one calorie of food, a plant-orientated diet is very economical. In order to produce one calorie of feedlot beef, ten calories of energy are required (which includes growing the animal feed, heating the barns, energy to run the feedlot, energy to dispose of animal waste, and energy for the slaughtering and packing operations). The corresponding figure for grass-fed beef and "factory-farmed" eggs is three calories; milk, 1 calorie; soya beans, 0.5; intensively grown corn and soya beans, 0.45; and intensively grown rice, only 0.15.

On a global scale, the overall energy savings are impressive. According to an article in *American Scientist,* an additional 29 million barrels of oil would have been needed by the year 2000 if the 1976 rate of meat consumption had continued. Because the demand for meat in the United States has slightly declined since 1976, a net saving of several million barrels of oil has already been realized.

For the most part, the conservation of energy seems to merit public attention only during an obvious shortage of oil or gas. However, from a viewpoint of ahimsa, energy conservation should always be a top priority. Whether or not energy supplies appear to be abundant at the moment, the conservation of non-renewable energy resources should be a long-term goal for everyone.

Living Simpler

Learning how to adopt a simple lifestyle offers a major opportunity to reduce one's energy consumption. In the home, improved insulation, more efficient heating and cooling systems, the installation of storm windows and doors, and reducing room temperatures in the winter (and wearing more warm clothing), using electricity only when needed, and avoiding energy-intensive appliances are just some of the basic ways to reduce domestic energy consumption.

Joining a car pool, driving only when absolutely necessary, taking public transportation and walking or cycling as often as possible will help conserve energy outside of the home. Buy reusable as opposed to disposable items. For example, you can bring a mug and table utensils to work rather than using styrofoam cups and plastic spoons, knives and forks. Maintain and repair products, like clothing, shoes and appliances, so that they won't have to be thrown out and replaced as frequently. Borrow, rent or share items that are used infrequently, like party decorations, tools or furniture. Buy used items as much as possible. Recycling paper, wood, clothing and glass will help reduce the consumption of energy in industry. In every aspect of life, energy conservation is one of the most creative and practical ways to help heal and protect our planet from destruction.

Green and Repurposed Buildings

Green, or sustainable, building is the practice of creating and using healthier and more resource-efficient models of construction, renovation, operation, maintenance and demolition. Green buildings share a number of common traits: they increase energy efficiency and especially the use of renewable energy; use water efficient fixtures and water systems; incorporate environmentally-friendly materials in construction and operation; highlight waste reduction and waste recycling; reduce toxic substances used in both construction and building operation; improve indoor air quality; and include eco-friendly landscaping. Green construction also features building design that is in harmony with the natural topographical features that surround the building site.

Using recycled materials in building construction is important, as well as finding ways to recycle buildings that already exist. Rather than focus on demolition and new construction, the goal is to renovate and repurpose buildings whenever possible. By utilizing the original superstructure and façade of a building, for example, the need for new materials can be reduced by more than half. Reusing elements such as floors and walls can also bring about significant savings.

As mentioned earlier, recycling construction materials can be carried out as well. For example, concrete granules from an old building can be reprocessed into concrete instead as sending it to a landfill site, and leftover masonry rubble can be re-used in the production of new masonry, such as bricks and concrete blocks.

Alternative Energies to Oil

Since the 1972-73 Arab oil embargo, efforts to develop alternative energy sources have increased on an unprecedented scale. In addition to coal, hydroelectric and nuclear power, renewable energy from the wind, trees and sun has received serious attention. In the following pages we will survey these major sources of energy, and examine both their benefits and impact on the Earth in the light of ahimsa.

Coal

Obtaining energy from coal has been of particular importance in Great Britain, North America, Russia and China, where it is found in large quantities. Unfortunately, the extraction and use of coal is expensive and often involves serious environmental damage to both the land and the air. The careful restoration of the land previously mined has been found to limit long-term damage to some extent, while improved pollution control devices can substantially reduce air pollution from coal-fired power plants.

Antipollution measures are not being applied in many plants located in developing nations. Acid rain from coal-fired plants and the threat of climate change through the greenhouse effect have been added to the range of coal-related ills and appear difficult to resolve through technological improvements alone.

Hydropower

Hydroelectric power has long been viewed as a dependable and pollution-free method for generating electricity. When compared to the costs for energy from coal and nuclear fission, hydroelectric power is less expensive, especially in Canada and the United States. Yet the construction of large dams has often produced serious environmental damage to rivers and surrounding land areas, and has wiped out entire human and nonhuman animal communities. Because hydropower is restricted to regions with large supplies of flowing water, the use of such power appears to be better suited for local use rather than on a national or even global scale.

Natural Gas

Natural gas occurs deep beneath the earth's surface. We use natural gas primarily to generate electricity, as well as for heating and transportation; it is also used to make materials and chemicals. Natural gas has many qualities that make it an efficient, relatively clean burning and economical energy source. However, there are environmental and safety issues that are associated with it.

Natural gas is made up primarily of methane, which is a greenhouse gas. Some natural gas leaks into the atmosphere from oil and natural gas wells, storage tanks, pipelines, and processing plants. The United States Energy Information Administration reports that these leaks were the source of about 29 percent of total U.S. methane emissions, and about 2 percent of total U.S. greenhouse gas emissions in 2013.

When a natural gas well is built on land, it requires an area to be cleared and leveled to host a pad where drilling takes place. Drilling activities produce air pollution and may disturb people, wildlife, and water resources. Pipelines are needed to transport the natural gas from the wells, which requires clearing land to bury the pipe. Natural gas production can also produce large amounts of contaminated water. This water has to be properly handled, stored, and treated so that it does not pollute nearby land and water.

In order to access the natural gas, energy companies often use a method that combines a form of horizontal drilling with hydraulic fracturing – more commonly known as *fracking*. This method blasts open fissures in underground shale-rock formations by injecting a high pressure combination of water, chemicals and proppants (a solid material, usually sand) that break up the shale and release the natural gas, which then flows to the production well.

The use of fluids for shale gas production can affect the availability of water for other uses, and can also affect aquatic habitats, such as wetlands, lakes and rivers. Hydraulic fracturing fluid—which often contains hazardous chemicals—can also be released by spills, leaks or faulty well construction. These releases can contaminate surrounding areas, including watersheds that provide drinking water to millions of people in cities even hundreds of miles away from a natural gas drilling site.

It is also well known that hydraulic fracturing causes earthquakes. Because fracking-related wastewater is often disposed of by injecting it into deep wells, it can cause earthquakes that are large enough to be felt and cause damage. In Oklahoma, a state with a history of seismic activity, the number of earthquakes increased as fracking became more prevalent. Oklahoma experienced 109 earthquakes with a magnitude of 3.0 or more on the Richter scale in 2013. This number increased to 579 in 2014 and 903 in 2015. The Oklahoma Geological Survey determined that the majority of these earthquakes were "very likely" triggered by the injection of wastewater into disposal wells. After the government finally established directives for wastewater disposal operators, the number of earthquakes in Oklahoma fell to 623 in 2016.

Nuclear Power

By far the most controversial alternative to oil-generated power has been that of nuclear fission. By the early 1970s, nearly two hundred nuclear power plants were built in the United States, Japan, the Soviet Union, Great Britain and the rest of Europe and India, while others are being planned and/or constructed in the Middle East, Asia and Latin America. By 1984- before the disastrous accident at the nuclear power plant near Chernobyl in the former Soviet Union- over 280 nuclear power plants had been built in nineteen countries, with over 500 plants in thirty countries expected to be in service by the end of the twentieth century.

The heart of a nuclear power plant is a unit of long, thin rods filled with pellets of uranium fuel. As uranium atoms are split within these fuel elements, energy is produced to heat water which is circulating through the reactor. This heated water produces steam that is carried to operate a turbine generator which in turn produces electricity.

From the beginning, representatives of government, industry and especially power companies were enthusiastic promoters of nuclear energy. Hailed as economical ("too cheap to meter"), reliable and safe, over 90 per cent of all monies for research and development for alternative energies to oil in the United States were devoted to nuclear energy, much at taxpayer and consumer expense. This figure is similar in the United Kingdom, where over £225 million was spent on nuclear research while only £14 million was devoted to research and development of non-nuclear energy sources. Since nuclear research began, many technological discoveries were made, and laws were passed to ensure the continued development and construction of nuclear plants around the world.

The 1972-73 oil crisis was widely seen as the final guarantee that power from nuclear fission would be the world's primary energy source. However, by the late 1980s, this view had changed substantially as construction costs for nuclear plants increased considerably while a wide variety of dangers from nuclear power generation began to come to light.

As evidenced by the much-publicized accidents at nuclear reactors on Three Mile Island, Pennsylvania in 1980, Chernobyl in 1986 and the Fukushima Daiichi disaster in 2011, the most obvious threat to life from nuclear reactors involves the possibility of a nuclear core meltdown.

A nuclear meltdown can occur if there is a malfunction in the reactor and the emergency cooling system does not work effectively. The radioactive core of the reactor would melt through the floor and begin to sink deep into the earth, where it can spread radioactivity through the water table to be eventually released above ground. A meltdown and explosion can also produce a major radiation release into the environment in which radioactive material in gaseous form would be scattered over a wide area.

In the case of Chernobyl, radioactive gas contaminated an area reaching as far away as Sweden and Scotland, affecting crops, livestock and water supplies. Medical officials have determined that this radioactive pollution will be responsible for premature death from cancer among thousands of people during the next sixty years. In addition, it is estimated that the area immediately surrounding the Chernobyl plant will be uninhabitable for centuries.

After the disaster at Fukushima, Germany accelerated plans to close its nuclear power reactors and decided to phase out nuclear power completely by 2022. Italy held a national referendum, in which 94 percent voted against the government's plan to build new nuclear power plants. In France, the president announced the government's intention to reduce nuclear usage by one third. And Taiwan – one of Japan's closest neighbors- stopped construction of a fourth nuclear power plant and expects to decommission the three existing ones by 2025.

In addition to the threat of radiation from an accident or terrorist attack, critics of nuclear power cite the increasing levels of thermal pollution that occur near nuclear plants, where water used for cooling the reactor is returned to the source whence it came at a higher temperature. As it heats up the river or lake, the oxygen levels of the water decrease and disrupt the natural balance of the entire ecosystem.

On a long-term basis it is feared that nuclear energy could eventually impair the global heat balance by releasing more heat into the atmosphere than the Earth receives from, and reflects back to, the Sun. Moreover, this effect could well be exacerbated by the increased levels of carbon dioxide in the atmosphere from car exhaust. A gradual overall rise in world temperature is already bringing about major climate change, disrupting agriculture, and causing the polar ice caps to melt, raising the level of the oceans and swamping low-lying land areas.

By far the most serious problem, however, concerns the safe disposal of radioactive waste from nuclear power plants. These wastes include strontium 90, cesium 137 and plutonium 269. They are all exceedingly toxic and pose a great threat to life for several hundred to many thousands of years.

For the most part, nuclear wastes are temporarily stored in tanks far from the reactor site and away from large population center. Transporting these wastes by road or rail is highly dangerous, and vulnerability from accident or terrorist attack is extreme.

Because leakage of radioactive wastes is a problem at temporary dumping sites, long-term projects include burying the waste in underground caves and salt beds, as well as beneath the ocean floor. Still, over osixty years after the development of commercial nuclear energy, there is yet much disagreement over how the tens of millions of gallons of radioactive waste can be stored in perpetuity.

The nuclear power industry is a big business, and has tremendous political, economic and social clout throughout the world. The initial planning and construction of a single nuclear reactor can involve up to $9 billion in materials, labor and technical expertise. Large corporations have a stake in nuclear power, as power companies can provide them with cheaper energy through special "high user" discounts. Politically, nuclear power plants tend to monopolize and concentrate energy resources, and make local communities overly dependent on large centralized regional and national power systems.

However, many of the incentives for building nuclear power plants do not take into account the high cost involved in disposing nuclear waste, nor the cost of the widespread contamination of land and people in the event of a nuclear accident. It is significant that when the construction of nuclear power plants first began in the United States, insurance companies would provide insurance for up to $65 million in case of an accident.

Their lack of confidence in the safety of nuclear reactors forced the government to pass the Price-Anderson Act in 1957, which would provide an additional $500 million in taxpayer-subsidized insurance. As of 2017, owners of nuclear power plants pay an annual premium for $375 million to private insurance companies for offsite liability coverage for each reactor site (not per reactor). This primary- or first tier- insurance is supplemented by a second tier, also paid indirectly by consumers. In the event that a nuclear accident causes damages in excess of $375 million, each licensee would be assessed a prorated share of the excess, up to $121.255 million per reactor. With 104 reactors in the insurance pool in 2017, this secondary tier of funds contained about $12.6 billion.

Yet even this amount would fall far short of the tens of billions of dollars in property claims and personal damages that can result from a nuclear reactor meltdown or other accident. If such a disaster ever occurs, Congress will have American taxpayers take care of the rest. In 2013, the Japanese Ministry of Economy, Trade and Industry (METI) calculated the costs of the Fukushima meltdowns at 11 trillion yen (¥), or approximately 102 billion U.S.

dollars. METI boosted its estimate after industry experts saw that decommissioning the wrecked Fukushima reactors alone would cost ¥8 trillion, which was quadruple an earlier estimate of ¥2 trillion.

Nuclear Fusion

There are several alternatives under study that can provide nuclear energy without some of the dangers inherent in nuclear fission. One such possibility is controlled nuclear fusion. Unlike fission, which involves the splitting of atoms, fusion combines two hydrogen nuclei to produce a chemical reaction which can be converted into useable energy.

Although viewed as somewhat less of a danger than nuclear fission, nuclear fusion is considered to be technically complex, financially costly, and politically and economically centralized. Thermonuclear fusion has a much lower power density than nuclear fission, which means that any fusion reactor needs to be larger and therefore more costly, than a fission reactor of the same power output. In addition, nuclear fission reactors use solid fuel which is denser than thermonuclear plasma, so the energy released is more concentrated.

Environmentalists point out that fusion reactors may take years to develop and will also involve the use of non-renewable energy sources. They are also linked to waste disposal problems, and can also be used to produce components for nuclear weapons.

These are some of the reasons why people like Dr. Helen Caldicott, a founder of Physicians for Social Responsibility, have been staunch opponents of nuclear power plants, whether of the fission or fusion variety.

Taking Action

Opposition to nuclear power has been expressed primarily though educational, legislative and legal channels. In addition, the use of nonviolent direct action against the construction of nuclear power plants has given a new dimension to the campaign for safe energy in Europe, Asia and North America.

The use of peaceful occupations of nuclear plant sites, blocking the entrances to construction areas, and submitting nonviolently to arrest are several of the most common methods of nonviolent direct action. Such activities demand careful training in the techniques of organization, strategy, communications and group dynamics. Each participant must be grounded in the fundamentals of civil disobedience so that their demonstration is not one of mere passivity.

There is also the need to understand the dynamics of the nuclear industry and to see the connection between nuclear power and related political, social, economic and environmental issues. Books like *Resource Manual for a Living Revolution* from New Society Publishers in the United States and *Manual for Action* from the Action Resources Group in London are excellent guides for those interested in nonviolent direct action.

Ahimsic Energy Alternatives

The use of non-nuclear energy sources holds tremendous promise. Utilizing renewable energy derived from wind, biofuels, geothermal energy and the Sun produces a relatively small amount of the world's electricity needs at the present time, with the bulk including coal, oil, natural gas and nuclear. As the requirements for safer energies increase, they will become more commercially viable.

According to the United States Energy Information Administration, non-nuclear renewable energy is expected to increase from 5 percent in 2012 to more than 14 percent by 2040.

Let's examine some of these alternative technologies and assess their capacity both to provide efficient energy and help protect the Earth and her inhabitants.

Wind Power

Harnessing the wind to generate electrical energy dates back to the 1890s. Wind generators were used throughout the rural United States during the first part of the twentieth century to electrify farms, and some are still used today in isolated parts of the United States, Canada and Australia. During the past few decades, hundreds of wind farms containing thousands of machines have been constructed in various parts of the world to generate electricity on a larger scale.

Results have been impressive. According to the U.S. Department of Energy, in 1990, California's wind power plants offset the emission of more than 2.5 billion pounds of carbon dioxide, and 15 million pounds of other pollutants that would have otherwise been produced. It would take a forest of 90 million to 175 million trees to provide the same air quality.

Modern wind turbines feature the latest in space-age materials, computerized controls and sophisticated transmissions systems. They currently supply millions of people with safe, renewable, pollution-free energy.

Wind power has some drawbacks, however. Bird and bat deaths are one of the most controversial biological issues related to wind turbines, although this problem is being addressed by better turbine location, new design protocols and other mitigation measures. The land available for large wind farms is often limited to sparsely populated areas that are hospitable to wind. Their "swooshing" sound has been disturbing to some neighbors, and many feel that the turbines themselves are unsightly. Yet the creation of wind farms has potential. Planners see more large-scale wind farms constructed offshore, while smaller projects can prove useful for more localized power consumption.

Biofuels

Wood is an abundant renewable energy resource found primarily in forest-rich countries in North America and Northern Europe. According to the Worldwatch Institute, millions of tons of wood waste and low-quality timber go unused every year in these countries and could, if properly utilized, sharply decrease the consumption of energy from coal, oil and nuclear fission.

Although clear-cutting vast areas of forests for fuel can hardly be justified in the light of ahimsa, the increased recovery and use of already available industrial waste wood, wood chips, bark and pulping wastes constitute both an economically and ecologically sound way to generate energy that is compatible with the goals of ahimsa.

Other methods of harvesting wood for fuel have drawn mixed reactions. The selective thinning and removal of old tree growth has been linked to an increase in new forest growth, but the systematic removal of leaves and twigs has been found to remove important nutrients that enhance forest growth. The future of harvesting wood for fuel is extremely uncertain, as the threat of acid rain from air pollution (primarily from industry, power plants and motor vehicle exhaust) is expected to take a major toll of forests in the coming years if present trends continue.

Finally, the burning of wood causes air pollution, a high percentage of which is believed to be toxic and carcinogenic. For this reason, many communities have restricted the use of wood-burning stoves or have required the use of catalytic converters. In addition to controlling wood pollutants, catalytic converters increase the efficiency of wood-burning stoves. Modern stoves certified by the U.S. Environmental Protection Agency (EPA) can reduce smoke emissions by up to 90 percent. They also include design features that promote secondary combustion aimed at burning off dangerous chemicals and toxic substances before they leave the firebox.

Biodiesel is made by combining alcohol (usually methanol) with vegetable oil, animal fat, or recycled cooking grease. It can be used as an additive (typically 20 percent) to reduce vehicle emissions. It can also be used in its pure form as an alternative fuel for diesel engines.

The National Renewable Energy Laboratory (NREL) in Colorado has been researching the production of liquid transportation fuels from microscopic algae. These microorganisms use the Sun's energy to combine carbon dioxide with water to create biomass more efficiently and rapidly than terrestrial plants. Oil-rich microalgae strains are able to produce the raw materials that form a number of transportation fuels, including "green" diesel, gasoline, biodiesel and jet fuel.

The controlled use of straw as fuel has also been advocated as a safe and economic way to produce energy, especially in the countryside. In Denmark, approximately one-quarter of all farms are heated with straw, which can be chopped and fed into a boiler or formed into fuel briquettes to be used in stoves.

Geothermal Energy

Geothermal energy comes directly from the Earth's vast storehouse of heat, which often escapes through hot springs, volcanoes, and geysers in many parts of the world. By the late 1980s, some twenty countries utilized geothermal energy for electricity, heating and cooling, saving the equivalent of nearly 100 million barrels of oil per year.

Geothermal energy is used in three major ways: using the earth's shallow ground for heating and cooking, generating electricity from the earth's heat, and producing heat directly from hot water within the earth. Geothermal energy is relatively economical when compared with coal, oil or nuclear energy. It has recently become a major growth industry, increasing at a rate of more than 10 per cent a year worldwide: some 214 trillion BTUs of energy are created by geothermal sources in the United States alone. With the more widespread use of pollution control devices to remove hydrogen sulfide (a noxious gas found at almost all geothermal sites) geothermal energy can be a promising ahimsic power source in future years.

Solar Energy

Solar energy appears to be the most viable of safe energy alternatives. It is found in abundance, it promotes self-reliance, and can be utilized for heating, cooling and for providing electricity. Solar photovoltaic cells are environmentally sound, relatively inexpensive (especially when compared to nuclear energy), and help to maintain the global heat balance. Solar energy provides many environmental, political and economic benefits and production is increasing at more than 25 percent a year. In the United States alone, the amount of energy generated by solar power increased from 225 trillion BTUs in 2013 to 427 trillion BTUs in 2015.

Solar technology is reliable, not easy to disrupt, sufficient for our needs, simple, low technology, transferable, flexible with respect to cultural and settlement patterns, and safe, with minimum environmental and climatic impacts. It produces free fuel, tends to resist commercial monopoly, has a high thermodynamic source potential (5,500 degrees K), is well matched to common energy-end uses and reduces international tensions arising from the uneven distribution of fuels and high technologies. It is also a spur to decentralization and local self- sufficiency, and helps to redress the severe energy imbalance between the temperate and tropical regions of the world.

Although more research needs to be done to further develop the capacity for the collection, storage and utilization of solar energy, government and private enterprise now realize that such research and development is worthy of their support and participation. As the world's most abundant and widespread energy source, the development of solar technology - especially in generating electricity - can have a dramatic impact on the quality of life of all the world's inhabitants. In addition to the potential economic, social and political benefits for human beings, solar energy will also go far in preserving the integrity of the global environment of which all planetary citizens are a part.

Developing safe, economically viable and environmentally sound energy technologies is a primary goal for those interested in ahimsa. According to the noted philosopher of science and systems theorist Ervin László:

> An energy technology that can accidentally
> kill large numbers of people, or be used to do
> so intentionally, is costly in human terms.
> One that can despoil the environment is
> costly in natural terms. And one that can
> eventually impair the heat balance of this
> planet may be suicidal for mankind, to say
> nothing of many other living species.

225

This is why our responsibility as human beings to conserve energy and to develop and utilize energy sources which enhance the well-being of all life on Earth is especially great at this time in our history. By becoming aware of safe energy alternatives to oil, coal and nuclear power, by urging their accelerated development and use, by making our views known to government and industry, by educating others to their benefits, and by using these energy sources in our own lives when possible, we will be fulfilling our role as planetary stewards. We will be aiding in the healing of the Earth Mother as we channel the powerful forces of energy to aid in the enhancement and evolution of all life for generations to come.

Part V

The Calling

A LIFE DEDICATED TO AHIMSA brings with it both great challenge and intense joy. Far from involving a superficial or partial goal in life, ahimsa signifies nothing less than a total personal commitment to acknowledging the unity of life, and the conscious desire to co-create with what Native Americans call the Great Spirit to build a world where evolution, harmony, unity and compassion guide the minds and hearts of humanity. It represents our desire to "come home" to our innermost essence where both intelligence and love can guide our lives.

Although a response to the call of ahimsa will begin a joyous and creative process in our lives, the path also contains many challenges and obstacles which may, at times, appear extremely difficult to overcome. In our work, we will have to become aware of many of our old images, beliefs and conclusions about ourselves, our family and friends, and the world that we have accepted since childhood. We will need to become aware of how we separate ourselves from others, and how we view problems confronting humanity that we feel are different from our own. We will need to confront the areas in us that are uncaring, lazy or indifferent, and deal with them with courage and decisiveness.

Since ahimsa also brings with it a greater awareness of our Higher Self, we will begin to recognize other, often neglected aspects of ourselves - our inner beauty, our deep compassion, our innate creativity, and our deep yearning for integration with ourselves and the world.

Whether we choose to live in the public eye or devote our energy to activities which are on a more personal scale, the active principle of dynamic compassion can fill us with a well-spring of enthusiasm, optimism and self-esteem which will be reflected in our health, our work and our relationships.

Chapter 13

Ahimsa and Right Livelihood

*When we accept the concept of right livelihood
as the basic right of all,
we shall have respect for each other.*

-The Holyearth Foundation

UNLIKE PHILOSOPHIES THAT TEACH that human
beings are merely the product of society, teachers of
ahimsa have maintained that we **create** society. By
manifesting the ideals of ahimsa in our daily lives, we can
gradually transform both the fabric and the dynamics of
society itself.

One of the most important areas for this
transformation to occur is in the workplace. On a
grassroots level, the essential goals of a company or
organization, its means of production, and the relationship
of the company to its workers can strongly affect their
personal lives. A company's actions will also have an
impact on the workers' families, the growth and direction

of related local businesses, and the well-being of the community as a whole.

On a larger scale, the product of services provided by the company or organization - whether it be insurance, plastic buttons or missile launchers - must have an impact on the economic, political and environmental life of the larger world community. The interdependence of nations for raw materials, the growth of transnational corporations, and the need to reach international markets require that we view the workplace as part of a global village in which the decisions and tasks we perform can have an impact - however subtle - on the well-being of the planet and its citizens. For this reason, we need to explore how, and to what extent, our working lives promote the ideals of ahimsa, or contribute to the store of greed, waste and violence in the world.

For the most part, we view our working life as something separate from our "real" life; that what we do at work has little or nothing to do with the rest of our daily existence. For many people, their bodies, minds and talents are merely rented to an employer for eight or more hours a day, five days per week, year after year. In exchange, they receive a salary and a number of benefits like health insurance and possibly several weeks of vacation per year. Upon retirement, they will probably receive a pension and a small token of appreciation - such as a watch - from the company.

The split between our working lives and our talents, interests and beliefs may be very dramatic and can be a source of tremendous personal conflict. On a primary level, it is a cause for boredom and frustration on the job, which can lead to depression, stress and anger. However, on an even deeper level, being in a job that does not resonate with our inner needs, talents and aspirations can erode our base of personal power. Because we may be working at a job that is at variance with our deepest beliefs, we may be contributing to the problems of the world rather than working to resolve them. As a result, we often experience inner cycles of guilt and resentment. Unless we are confronted with a dramatic event - such as a severe illness or layoff, we can maintain such negative cycles for many years without making a decisive effort to break out of them.

This is why the choice of one's means of livelihood is one of the most important decisions an individual can make. And when we seek to govern our lives according to the laws of ahimsa, our personal choices regarding career are all the more vital.

Right Means of Livelihood

The concept of right means of livelihood was first introduced to the world by the Buddha, and is considered one of the eight primary directions to follow -known as *The Noble Eightfold Path**- in order to bridge the threshold of self-realization and spiritual liberation. A contemporary definition of right means of livelihood appeared in Mark Gerzon's article about New Age entrepreneurs in *The New York Times*:

> Right livelihood means that work should not
> only provide a living but also develop
> selfhood, foster companionship and nourish
> the earth. If a business makes money but
> alienates its members from one another, from
> themselves and from nature, it is a livelihood
> - but it is not a right livelihood.

*The Noble Eightfold Path includes Right Knowledge, Right Thought, Right Speech, Right Activity, Right Means of Livelihood, Right Exertion, Right Memory and Right Concentration.

According to Danaan Perry and Lila Forest in *The Earthsteward's Handbook,* right livelihood needs to encompass all of the following aspects of one's life:

-produce something of personal benefit rather than just material benefits to others;
-provide a fair return which fulfils one's personal needs while not encouraging personal greed;
-give us a sense of being a valued part of the local and larger community;
-develop a touchstone of deep experience by which to measure other situations in life;
-provide genuine personal satisfaction and self-fulfillment;
-increase skill and the development of one's talents and faculties; and
-give expression to the values by which one lives.

In the context of ahimsa, a right means of livelihood would not only satisfy these basic needs, but would encourage harmony, peace, and co-operation as well. Rather than merely providing us with a means to ensure our financial security and social position, a right means of livelihood would help bring about self-acceptance, self-esteem and self-discovery. It would gently inspire the delicate process of healing ourselves as well as the members of the larger community. As a result, the health of the entire planet is enhanced, and we create the conditions which permit a more compassionate and peaceful world to take shape.

At this point in our history, the possibilities for choosing a right means of livelihood have never been so varied and exciting. Years ago, when people only worked to survive, professional choices were often limited, especially among women. For men, agriculture, factory work, and sales made up the bulk of available careers. In many cases, children followed in the professional footsteps of their parents, despite whatever talents and interests they may have had.

Today, however, such limitations need no longer exist. With the stunningly rapid growth of new technologies, vast new areas for career choice have opened up. Work in the environmental protection field, career possibilities in "soft-power" technologies like solar, wind, hydro and steam, work involving communication, alternative healing, social science, occupational therapy, teaching, politics, the arts, sales and other service-orientated professions offer many possibilities for right livelihood as we have entered the twenty-first century.

Embracing the Core

Yet even among students of ahimsa there is controversy over what exactly constitutes right livelihood. Traditionally, jobs involving the raising, slaughter and sale of animals for meat or fur, production and sale of weapons, and work as a soldier, tobacco vendor or purveyor of alcohol or harmful drugs have not been considered right means of livelihood. Any work whose success depends on the suffering of other people would not be considered right means of livelihood either. However, jobs involving healing, fire-fighting, growing vegetables and fruit, art, teaching or religion were all considered benign and peaceful, and were more likely to fall within the definition of right means of livelihood.

In our increasingly complex society of computer technology and fiber optic communication, such arbitrary distinctions tend to be no longer useful. Although some traditional classifications - such as those of weapons manufacturer or butcher - may still be valid, others which were formerly considered to be acceptable may no longer be applicable to modem life. For this reason, it is important to examine both the goals and methods involved in a particular type of work in order to arrive at a fair evaluation.

The advertising industry, for example, is essentially benign. In its pure form, the function of advertising is to provide consumers with factual information about available products and services. Through education, advertising is designed to help the public make intelligent choices regarding the goods and services they need.

But as we all know, advertising has been a form of either subtle or blatant manipulation, whose main function is to persuade us to buy what we do not really need. By appealing to greed, fear, status and other appearance values, modem advertising has been largely responsible for creating the demand for the staggering amount of disposable goods and shoddy products which produce the waste, consumer indebtedness and environmental pollution that are hallmarks of twentieth-century consumer society.

On the other hand, advertising has also been very effective in promoting environmental protection, world peace, animal welfare, and taking personal responsibility for one's health. Advertising that alerts teenagers and others to the dangers of drug abuse, alcoholism, smoking, unwanted pregnancy, and diseases like HIV/AIDS has proven extremely valuable and instructive.

With this in mind, perhaps it is more useful to focus on the essential *keynote quality* of each profession, and consider how this essential quality - if benign - can be either distorted to promote wastefulness, chaos and greed in the world, or can be deepened, purified and enhanced so that it can be a potent channel for ahimsa.

Making Choices

Exercising one's *ability to choose* is essential to this process. My father, for example, worked as an electronics engineer, an essentially benign profession, but with strong links to the defense industry. Although most of his financial security could have resulted from working at projects that were related to the military, my father decided at one point in his career to get involved in exclusively non-military work. His decision involved much professional risk, but he was able to find an appropriate position after only a few months.

Decisions such as this may create enormous personal and professional challenges. In some cases, they may lead to our having to redefine the meaning of the word "success." In our present violent and wasteful society, much emphasis is placed on the outer symbols of success: having the right car, home or country club membership, being installed in the corner office or having an impressive professional title, owning glamorous stocks and wearing this season's popular fashions.

When we make the choice for right means of livelihood in the light of ahimsa, the idea of success goes beyond appearances: it involves aligning our outer activities with our deepest and most cherished goals and aspirations. Although the decision to adopt a right means of livelihood may -though not necessarily- bring about the collapse of many of the outer, more acknowledged forms that society terms "successful," we move closer to the essence of personal satisfaction and self-fulfillment that constitute the real meaning of success.

Whether we are involved in the fields of engineering, sales, manufacturing, writing, food service, design, counseling, art or education, we need to consider how the nature and goals of our work reflect its benign "core quality" - which by definition promotes right livelihood - or if we are contributing towards furthering violence, waste, pollution, alienation and the attachment to greed and appearance values.

As mentioned earlier, it is impossible to avoid all himsa in daily life, and our livelihood is no exception. Even though much my father's work involved inventing safety devices for civilian aircraft, there was no guarantee that the warning system he developed for a passenger plane would not eventually be used in a military fighter. The post office employee whose essentially benign (and extremely important) job facilitating communication among people of the world may also sort or deliver material that can promote violence, waste or greed.

Even in producing a "hard copy" book about ahimsa, trees are destroyed, the glue made to bind the pages may have been taken from animal by-products, while delivery of the book to shops by truck involves air and noise pollution. For this reason, we need to work to avoid work-related himsa *as much as possible* while seeking to enhance and manifest the essentially benign core qualities our work or profession contains.

Honesty and Compassion

An otherwise right means of livelihood can also be distorted by dishonesty, greed and unfair business practices. If a dentist, for example, recommends a dental procedure with the primary goal of making more money, he is no longer practicing a right means of livelihood. When a store owner sells poor-quality goods, or promotes items that contribute to waste, wealth addiction or appearance values, his or her goal of right livelihood is severely compromised. When an author, journalist or blogger indulges in sensationalism, fake news or otherwise misleads or misinforms readers, he or she is not practicing a right means of livelihood.

In our dealings with the world as teachers, doctors, clerks, waiters, taxi drivers, machinists or homemakers, we are relied upon to be trusted, to be truthful. When we do not live up to normal expectations of honesty and trust in whatever profession we hold, we are not practicing right means of livelihood. We are eroding the essential values that make up the foundations of ahimsa.

Compassion in our professional lives is equally, if not more, important. A landlord who shows genuine concern for her tenants, a teacher who takes the time to listen to the problems of his students, or a grocer or restaurant owner who donates unsold food to community kitchen - all are taking important steps towards practicing a right means of livelihood.

When the spirit of compassion is integrated into our daily working lives, we help create benign cycles of peace and healing which go beyond our immediate sphere of influence. By making a firm daily commitment to serving as a channel for ahimsa before we begin our daily tasks, we can transform our relationship to work, and help make the goal of ahimsa more of a reality in our life.

Perhaps one of the most moving statements about integrating ahimsa into one's career was made by Dr. Yeshi Donden, a Buddhist monk and physician to the Dalai Lama for twenty years, during an interview with a reporter from *The New York Times Magazine:*

> Compassion is the special prerequisite of being a doctor. In my own life, the more I have seen of suffering, the more I have come to feel compassion. I am an ordinary person affected by desire, hatred and ignorance. I can't make any claims. But whatever I do, I do my best to make love and compassion the center of my motivation.

Out in Public

Perhaps the most potent opportunities for furthering ahimsa are available for those who work with the public. Waiters, taxi and bus drivers, police officers, hotel and motel workers, salespeople, flight attendants, teachers, actors, social workers, counselors, customer service workers, postal service employees, health-care workers, plumbers, delivery people, performing artists and bank clerks are privileged in their professions to be able to express compassion, kindness and truth to others face-to-face during every single day of their working lives.

Because these people can interact with dozens or even hundreds of people each day, the opportunities for sharing the essence of ahimsa are plentiful indeed. And in a society where plastic smiles, empty speech and routine dishonesty often prevail, a sincere and focused commitment to express our innate caring and compassion can have a potent ripple effect on others. The seeds we plant each day can all help in the healing of our planet and help make ahimsa more of a concrete reality in the world.

Sowing the seeds of ahimsa are not restricted to those who work with the public. For the business person or entrepreneur, for example, there is a pressing need to provide goods and services that will promote co-operation, selfhood and planetary healing. In an age characterized by rapid technological growth, innovative entrepreneurs can create new products, programs and services that can help us to realize the goals of ahimsa in our generation. For the business person, special attention can be given to ways to maintain the highest standards of integrity and compassion, while promoting the personal growth of those involved with the business itself. The ideal of service, dedication and responsiveness to one's employees, clients, neighbors and suppliers can do much towards expressing the ideal of ahimsa in everyday life.

For those who are creative, their skills and imagination can be channeled towards serving humanity and the world rather than fostering superficiality, appearance values, and acquisitiveness. In his excellent book *Compassion,* Matthew Fox characterized the creativity that goes into silver money clips, for example, as decadent creativity, because it is luxury-orientated rather than people-orientated. It promotes living "on the periphery" rather than encouraging people to go deeper within themselves and to satisfy their genuine needs. Whether we are artists, advertising executives, interior designers, architects, products designers, scientists or investors, the challenge of utilizing our innate talents-which can affect the lives of many- to further the goals of ahimsa is especially great at this time in human history. For it is through true creativity that positive changes can take place, and it is through the vision of the truly creative that others can learn and grow.

The goal of right means of livelihood is not reserved for the few. It is not restricted to those who are independently wealthy, nor to those who have the "right" jobs, like the teacher, the monk or the healer.

Whether we need to work in order to put food on the table, or are able to work on a voluntary basis, we must be willing to acknowledge our own personal choices: not only regarding our choice of profession, but how we create our own reality *within* our chosen profession or career.

By acknowledging our own responsibility, we are able to get more in touch with our personal power. We can begin to tap the part of us which knows what is true and what is right, and how this truth and compassion can be expressed in our daily working lives.

Chapter 14

Ahimsa and Inner Healing

*People ought not to consider so much what they are to do
as what they are;
let them be good and their ways and deeds will shine
brightly.*

-Meister Eckhart

AHIMSA TEACHES THAT LASTING HAPPINESS lies in
the discovery of our deepest and most beautiful human
qualities: intelligence, justice and compassion. It adheres
to the universal law which states that like produces like,
order comes out of order, and peace can only be achieved
through peace. The teachings of ahimsa maintain that in
life situations, the ends and means are one and the same,
and that truth, honesty and compassion must make up the
foundation for one's personal actions in any truly civilized
society.

240

Because we cannot live our lives in separated watertight compartments, our personal thoughts, attitudes, modes of behavior and even our physical state of being inevitably project onto the whole structure and direction of society at large.

When we ourselves lack integration, wholeness and alignment, whether through guilt, destructive attitudes or wrong belief, we are at war with ourselves, and our physical and emotional health will suffer as a result.

Throughout this book, we have explored how the philosophy and practice of ahimsa can transform the fabric of society and help create a peaceful and compassionate world. However, if the power of ahimsa does not penetrate into our deepest inner selves, it cannot be effectively manifested in the daily outer reality of our lives. It just won't happen.

This is why we need to remember that ahimsa towards others must go hand in hand with ahimsa towards oneself. Because ahimsa teaches that we should treat ourselves as we would our most cherished relatives and friends, our philosophy of love and compassion cannot only be expressed in an outward sense towards others, but must also be a daily blessing which we give to ourselves.

By choosing to receive the gift of inner healing from the universe, we co-operate in building the groundwork for healing the human community. Because each of us are, in the words of Peace Pilgrim, a "cell in the body of humanity," the health of the whole begins with the health of each individual member on physical, emotional and spiritual levels. By working to achieve a state of dynamic health and wholeness in our own lives, we cannot help projecting that healthfulness to others.

Outgoing, Incoming

However, many people - especially those who are serious by nature - have difficulty receiving inner healing. In most cases, we feel called primarily to "do the work" and attend to the needs of others first, before we concentrate on our own personal needs. Campaigning for animal rights, working for nuclear disarmament, helping the elderly or the homeless, or coordinating a recycling program are all extremely important and deserve our energy, talent and commitment. In a world of violence and despair, there is a tremendous need for intelligent, dynamic and compassionate individuals who can - whether at home, at work, or through political and social action - work to transform the present spirals of violence into benign cycles of co-operation and harmony.

In addition to becoming aware of the need for active involvement with the outer world, we also must become conscious of any inner currents - whether attitudes or thoughts - which may lead us to resist "giving unto ourselves" as we wish to give to others. Feelings of guilt, the belief that we are somehow undeserving of love, kindness and pleasure, or a rigid focus on the need to do only what is "useful" are some of the barriers to receiving inner healing.

Although we cannot explore these issues in great depth here, it is important to examine them nevertheless. By gradually becoming aware of destructive attitudes, anger, or residual guilt feelings from past events, we can place them in the context of our present- day reality. By holding these old beliefs, attitudes and feelings up to the light, we can gain new understanding. As a result, we can become more open to feeling that we deserve the best that the universe has to offer. Like love, beauty and affection, the healing energy of the universe is available in *unlimited* quantities. The more we are able to tap for ourselves, the more we can channel outwardly to others.

Forgiveness

Although there are many areas of importance to explore, forgiveness as an essential aspect of inner healing cannot be stressed enough. The unforgiving mind views the actions of others as sins rather than as mistakes, and it sees others as evil who do not have the desire or capacity to change. Because the unforgiving mind sees little difference between the "sin" and the "sinner," it closes the door to compassion and understanding, while it strengthens - or even crystallizes - our own sense of injury or personal injustice.

Holding on to past hurts, old grievances and judgments about others creates disharmony and strengthens the illusion of separateness. Because our judgments of others are often a reflection of our own feelings towards unresolved issues and difficulties we find in ourselves, our not forgiving others reinforces our own sense of personal guilt and feelings of unworthiness.

In our society, guilt often implies punishment, and when we feel guilty for not forgiving, or for withholding our understanding and compassion, we mobilize the currents within that thrive on conflict and fear. The lack of alignment that results causes internal "dis-ease" that can lead to actual physical illness. Our self-esteem is eroded, and we are unable to mobilize the innate forces of self-healing we need to become whole once more.

Forgiveness does not imply that we dispense charity to others while maintaining an aura of superiority of self-importance. Rather, it stems from a realization of our own identification with the person who hurt us, along with the knowledge that we could be capable of the same offence.

We may also wish to recall our own present and past offences towards ourselves and others, and feel the need to be forgiven for them and to make restitution.

From this place of humility and respect, we can see our adversary in a different light. While we need not forget the offence, we can transform our anger and hurt into a state of compassionate understanding. In the words of William Quan Judge, one of the founders of The Theosophical Society:

> Entire charity, constant forgiveness, wipes
> out the opposition from others, expends the
> old enmity and at the same time makes no
> new similar causes. Any other sort of thought
> or conduct is sure to increase the sum of hate
> in the world, to make cause for sorrow, to
> continually keep up the crime and misery in
> the world. Each man can for himself decide
> which of the two ways is the right one to
> adopt.

According to Richard Smoley, author of the acclaimed book *The Deal: A Radical Guide to Complete Forgiveness*, forgiving others is not always an easy process that brings immediate results. In an article appearing in *Quest* magazine, he wrote:

> A practical approach toward forgiveness may
> involve fostering a small willingness to
> forgive while anger and rage burn themselves
> out for weeks or months. It may require
> drawing a line with someone—refusing to
> take any more abuse while also refusing to
> nurture any hatred on account of it.
> Frequently it necessitates an inner
> detachment, a freedom from emotional

dependence on others. Sometimes it entails looking at the situation from the other people's perspective... Forgiveness takes forms as diverse and unpredictable as human beings themselves. For some, generous and high-minded, it comes naturally and spontaneously, while others may find that it has to be cultivated with effort in the hard soil of their natures. It's wise to be honest with ourselves about such things, but it's also wise to remember that forgiveness is to be bestowed inwardly as well as outwardly and that a little mercy granted to ourselves often makes it easier to extend this kindness to others.

A Forgiveness Meditation

The following meditation is designed to help facilitate forgiveness.

1. Sit comfortably. If you are sitting on a mat, cross your legs; if you are sitting on a comfortable hard-backed chair, place your feet flat on the floor. Your spine should be straight, your shoulders relaxed, and your eyes should be positioned straight ahead. Fold your hands lightly in your lap or place them, palms up, on your thighs.

2. Gently close your eyes. Be aware of your breathing, which should be from the diaphragm. Don't try to control your breathing, but be aware of its rhythm. Maintain awareness on your breath for a few moments.

3. When your body is fully relaxed and aware of itself, bring your attention back to your breath for a few moments.

4. Now bring to mind someone who has wronged you recently, and whom you have not yet forgiven.

5. Review the unpleasant exchange or situation as it occurred, without exaggerating or otherwise altering any element.

6. Gently ask yourself the following questions:

   a. How might this exchange have occurred in a more positive way?
   b. What could I have said (or not said) or done (or not done) to have produced a different result?
   c. How might I have contributed to the problem due to feelings of pride, fear or self-will?
   d. How might the other person have responded to any positive gestures on my part?

7. At this point, take a few deep breaths, and say aloud: "I wish to forgive, as I wish to be forgiven".

8. Allow yourself to feel compassion and forgiveness for the person, even if it is just a small amount of forgiveness at first (this meditation can be repeated whenever you wish).

9. Then take a few more deep breaths, slowly open your eyes, and return to everyday reality once more.

If you can, communicate with that person and offer your forgiveness. As a result of the meditation, you may also want to ask for forgiveness yourself, since you may have discovered that you contributed to the unpleasant situation.

By striving to see the good in the other person (however hidden it may appear at first), we strengthen our own image of innate goodness. By extending our forgiveness towards others from the heart, we create a benign cycle of release, relinquishment, and generosity. In time, the ongoing practice of forgiving will enable us to realign our minds and emotions with our spiritual centre or "core". As a result, we can tap the innate forces of healing that exist both inside and outside our bodies, and restore ourselves to the state of vibrant emotional, mental and physical health we deserve.

Embracing Earth Energy

Another important aspect of inner healing involves opening ourselves to what Native Americans Indians call *Earth energy*. Communing with nature is perhaps the most effective way to do this.

When we experience the beauty of a waterfall, the majesty of a tree or the colors of a field of flowers, most of us have perceived "something else" that goes beyond the five senses: feelings of peace, comfort, healing, and protection. Many of us have come back from a walk in the woods with new inspiration, unexpected solutions to difficult problems, and fresh insights into our life and relationships.

Appreciating Trees

Trees are finally becoming recognized for the valuable life-affirming services they provide. In an age when one's worth is based largely on what we create and produce, trees perform many valuable tasks that are essential for our survival.

1. Trees provide the oxygen we need to live. One hectare (approximately 2.5 acres) of mature forest produces

thirty tons of oxygen annually: enough to satisfy the oxygen needs of 300 humans for an entire year.

2. They also absorb many of the chloroflourocarbons (CFCs) which destroy the ozone layer that surrounds the planet, and remove particulates and gases from the atmosphere, including carbon dioxide, one of the major causes of the green-house effect and modifying weather patterns.

3. In addition to providing food and shelter for wildlife, trees give shade to our homes and businesses, thus reducing the use of fans and air conditioners in the summer months by up to 40 percent. Trees planted by rivers, lakes and streams keep water temperatures low so that fish can spawn, grow and thrive.

4. Trees not only fertilize the land, but they prevent soil erosion by holding it together with their often complex and abundant root systems.

5. Their roots also absorb water, helping to prevent mudslides during strong rains.

6. By serving as aerodynamic windbreaks in many agricultural areas, trees (such as the Lombardy poplar) protect the integrity of the soil and reduce soil loss and crop destruction due to wind activity.

Making Friends with Trees

The prominent American tree culturist P.G. Cross wrote of the value of developing close personal relationships with trees almost a century ago:

If you would live life in all its richness, then make friends with your trees, your neighbor's trees, the trees of the hillside and the highway. To form such a friendship means serenity of being, better health, and above all, lasting happiness. No tree ever proves to be a false friend.

Though few of us realize it consciously, we have always been chemically, genetically, emotionally and physiologically linked to trees. As providers of food (such as fruits, leaves, bark, nuts and berries) the genetic essence of trees has been ingested by humans throughout our evolution, and thus has become chemically an integral part of our bodies.

In addition, the water from fruit has become the water in our bodies, an ingredient in every single organ and tissue. The oxygen that the tree produces through photosynthesis is taken into our lungs and becomes- like water- a part of every single body cell. This not only occurs when we take a breath of air or drink a glass or orange juice, but has been passed down to us genetically through hundreds of generations.

This intimate and powerful link between humans and trees has always existed on the most primal of levels, yet it is still largely unrecognized and acknowledged. A major task of humanity is to humbly take account of this forgotten reality, and see how it can lead us towards a change in consciousness to reclaim our union with trees and other plants, and thus lead us towards protecting and defending them from harm.

Those who are concerned with the tremendous deforestation taking place throughout the world feel that we must begin to view the concept of "trees as relations" not as a religious theory put forth by mystics and shamans, but as *scientific fact*. This approach calls for a different focus, a more inclusive attitude, and a more encompassing world view. If each of us can begin to identify with trees as family and friends, our relationship with the natural world begins to shift. As a result, making peace with nature can become a reality in our lifetime.

Tree Communion: Some Personal Strategies

Perhaps the most important key to tree communion will be the conscious awareness and recognition of trees and the important role they play in our survival and evolution. Part of this process is to begin to acknowledge what we have long taken for granted. When we walk across a room, we can remind ourselves that the floor upon which we walk is made from trees; when we sit down for dinner, we can remind ourselves that the dining table and chair are made from the bodies of trees; that our evening newspaper is part of a tree; that our rayon shirt or blouse is made from trees; or that the apple or pear we enjoy for dessert is the living fruit of a generous tree.

By the same token, we can begin to acknowledge the aesthetic and spiritual impact that trees have on our lives. When we leave the house each morning, how many of us truly see the trees in our midst? How many of us are aware of their beauty, their grace, and their strength? By becoming more consciously aware of the many gifts we have received from trees in daily life, we begin to feel gratitude and respect, which open the door to actual communion.

There are a wide variety of pleasurable activities that can bring us closer to trees. Visiting their natural habitats and carefully observing them, taking photographs of or drawing them, speaking to trees, relaxing in their shade, listening to their moving branches or the rustling of their leaves, touching or hugging trees and meditating under their boughs.

This appreciation can lead to a number of concrete strategies to promote the welfare of trees. One simple idea involves informally "adopting" a tree on a local street or in a park, and look after its welfare. In addition to protecting the tree from dogs or vandals, regular watering may be needed during periods of drought, especially if the tree is recently planted. Have people been dumping garbage around the tree? Clean it up. Did someone staple a sign to the tree to announce a yard sale? Remove the sign and the staples. Is the tree in need of repair? Notify the proper local authorities or have your neighbors join in subsidizing the costs of the necessary care.

Finally, learn to simply enjoy the company of a tree. Lie down under its boughs. Enjoy a picnic in its shade. Lean against the tree if you are tired, allowing your back to align with its trunk. Embrace a tree with both arms. If you are sad or are dealing with a personal problem, sit by a tree and ask for help; many find that the grounded energy of a tree helps us to develop focus and calm. And if you wish to gain natural wisdom, meditate under a tree or pray under its branches. Communion with trees– even for a few minutes– can help us reconnect to the natural world, and provide the groundedness and inner security that is our birthright as human beings.

A Suggested Tree Meditation

Humans have been meditating in the presence of trees for millennia. Although there are many different ways to meditate, the following basic method   can be easily modified according to your personal needs and goals.

1. Find a comfortable place under (or near) a tree where you can be quiet and alone.

2. Select a comfortable position. Some may prefer sitting in a chair under a tree, while others would rather sit in a

cross-legged position on a cushion or rug. You can also lean against the tree trunk or lie down on the ground.

3. If you prefer to meditate with eyes open, select something simple to focus your eyes upon, like a tree trunk, leaf or branch. This will keep your mind from wandering. If you keep your eyes closed, try to visualize a field of white light.

4. Begin to breathe slowly and deeply, becoming aware of your breath as it enters and leaves your body. Each time your mind wanders to other thoughts or is disturbed by outside noises, gently bring your attention back to the easy, natural rhythm of your breathing. If you have trouble keeping your mind on your breath, count each inhalation and exhalation up to ten, and then start over again.

5. As you relax physically, you may find that various feelings come and go. They shouldn't be repressed, but the very act of calmly observing them may cause them to gradually lose their intensity.

6. Gradually intuit and then visualize the concept of oneness with the tree. Express your desire to experience the reality of oneness an integral part of your life today, either in silence or out loud: "I pray to realize my oneness with nature today". Repeat this visualization slowly several times. You can also express other desires or yearnings you have which you want to integrate into your life during the day. This process is akin to "sending a letter of intent to the universe".

7. After having expressed your keynote visualization, relax and be receptive once more. Continue your relaxed, deep breathing for at least three minutes and feel the sense of oneness living inside your body, near the heart. Feel it

streaming out towards the tree, into the woods, into your neighborhood, and further out into the world. End your meditation gradually and in silence. Giving thanks to the tree directly, in the form of an embrace or a verbal expression of gratitude, is encouraged!

Eating for Life

In an earlier chapter we discussed the merits of a compassionate diet, and how eating low on the food chain reduces cruelty to animals, is good for the environment, and has the potential for feeding far more people than a diet containing animal products. While advocates of ahimsa have championed diets which contain a minimum of animal products, there is little consensus regarding recommendations for specific diets, which run the gamut from strict macrobiotics to natural hygiene.

The totally fruitarian diet is probably the diet most consistent with the goals of ahimsa. Fruits picked from local orchards, "fruity" vegetables like eggplant and squash that do not involve killing the plant, and locally harvested nuts and seeds constitute the most harmless of human diets, but require a thorough grounding in the essentials of human nutrition. Other pure vegetarian diets are less nutritionally restrictive, and can be enjoyed by people living in nearly every area of the world. Because there are literally hundreds of diets and people have very specific needs, we are not about to recommend any specific diet here.

However, as a general guideline, progressive nutritionists have suggested that the best kinds of foods for the body are those that are fresh and unrefined, such as fresh (as opposed to frozen or canned) fruits and vegetables, whole and raw seeds, nuts and grains. Fats, salt and sugar should be kept to a minimum, as should heavily processed foods like white flour products, white rice and margarine.

Lanza del Vasto, an associate of Mahatma Gandhi, offered some good nutritional advice in his book *Make Straight the Way to the Lord:*

> To eat well is to take food that strengthens,
> refreshes and leaves the head clear; food that
> does not bemuse the intelligence, excite,
> bum, or weigh on the stomach. It means
> taking the fruits of the earth you are living on
> when nature offers them; putting as little
> space and time as possible between the earth
> and your mouth; preparing them with the
> least artifice possible; presenting them raw or
> cooking them over a gentle heat. It means
> restoring your health and strength first from
> the brown bread of the earth, the grey salt of
> the sea, and olive oil and honey from the sun.

How we treat food is also important. When we prepare our meals, we should do so with a sense of gratitude and respect. Before we eat, blessing our food is recommended for a number of reasons. It not only is an expression of thanks to the Earth Mother for giving us nourishment, but it brings us into a greater state of resonance with the food itself. We also bring ourselves to a state of inner calm, which is essential for good digestion and the increased assimilation of vital nutrients.

When we become more attuned to the food we eat, we are more likely to consume "just enough" to fulfill our real dietary needs. As a result, we derive greater pleasure from eating, yet we are less likely to abuse our bodies through overeating, eating too quickly, or indulging in other unhealthy habits related to food.

Stress and Ahimsa

For many soldiers of ahimsa who involve themselves in the world, constructively dealing with the stresses of everyday life can be a major challenge. A hundred years ago, people had few problems with stress. Life was far less complex than it is today, and most tension could be dealt with by performing strenuous physical work - like chopping wood or baling hay - or other simple activities like quilting, milking the cows or harvesting vegetables.

According to Hans Selye, M.D., author of *Stress Without Distress,* stress is a normal part of life, and involves the *body's response to any demand made on it.* While a family argument can be a source of stress, so can a pleasurable experience like watching a sunset. Dr. Selye and others have believed that our ability to adapt to stress is a key to good health. When we are unable to adapt, we are in *distress,* which is linked to a wide variety of emotional and physical problems like hypertension, depression, heart disease and even cancer.

There are a variety of healthy - and enjoyable - ways to deal with the stresses of daily life, such as going for a walk or a run, enjoying music, dancing, participating in a sport, reading a book or working in a garden. Laughter is also an important aspect of stress-reduction and inner healing. In his book *Anatomy of an Illness,* political journalist and world peace advocate Norman Cousins told how ten minutes of belly laughter at frequent intervals (he watched Marx Brothers movies and old "Candid Camera" reruns) helped him overcome a life-threatening illness. While humor shouldn't be used as a total escape from life, or be indulged in at the expense of others, integrating humor and "laugh therapy" into our daily lives can help relieve tension during or after stressful periods of the day.

Other pleasurable ways to deal with daily tension include giving and receiving at least four hugs a day, having a massage at least once a week, devoting one day a week completely to "play" (i.e. a totally enjoyable and non-productive activity), and spending at least fifteen minutes per day on physical exercise, such as aerobics.

Although some of these suggestions may appear to be frivolous at first glance, they reflect a deeper, more serious intent to promote relaxation, harmony and greater energy. They help us create the conditions for inner healing to take place.

We can also reduce stress by creating a healing environment in the home. Being surrounded by plants, healing colors, and harmonious music are all conducive to relaxation and contribute to our sense of well-being. If at all possible, we should have a special room as a personal sanctuary, where we can think, meditate or merely be alone. Rock crystals (such as clear quartz or amethyst) are known for their healing properties and their ability to help us to relax when we hold them or carry them as jewelry.

Simply Relax

One of the most effective ways to deal with stress involves the selective tensing up and relaxing of the voluntary muscles of the body. Although not measured by scientific instruments until recently, the benefits of such relaxation include a decrease in muscle tension, heartbeat, oxygen consumption, blood-pressure and respiratory rate. While different methods of progressive relaxation have been introduced in books like *The Relaxation Response* and *Getting Well Again* (see Bibliography), the following relaxation technique is both simple and effective, and can be practiced almost anywhere.

1.   First, tense the muscles in your face, and hold this tension for a few seconds. Then completely relax.

2.   Now gradually move down your neck and tense the muscles. Then completely relax.

3.   Repeat this exercise in different sections of the body by working down through the shoulders, arms, hands, chest, stomach, buttocks, legs and feet. By the time you reach your feet, a relaxed state will almost surely result.

4.   As a variation, all the muscles of the body can be tensed and then relaxed at the same time, or a particular muscle can be tensed, relaxed, and gently massaged.

5.   When you release tension, you can 'let your breath out', accompanied by a long "aaahh" or a sigh. This will assist your getting in touch with your deeper feelings and will help you release them.

6.   Quiet, deep breathing can follow this exercise, and you can give more attention to any parts of the body which require additional relaxation.

Meditating for Peace

Meditating for peace not only sends strong emanations of love and unity out into the world, it mobilizes the powerful forces of self-healing and harmony within. While there are many techniques for peace meditation, most of them share at least four basic elements: quiet surroundings, a comfortable position, an object or concept to focus upon, and a receptive attitude. The following method is but one of many possibilities, and can be modified according to personal needs and goals.

1.   Find a comfortable place where you can be quiet and alone for a short time each day.

2.   Select a comfortable position. Some may prefer sitting in a chair, while others would rather sit in a cross-legged position on a cushion or rug.

3.   For those who meditate with their eyes open, select something simple to focus your eyes upon, like a candle, a flower, a religious symbol or other beautiful object. This will keep your mind from wandering. If you keep your eyes closed, try to visualize a field of white light.

4.   Begin to breathe slowly and deeply, becoming aware of your breath as it enters and leaves your body. Each time your mind wanders to other thoughts or is disturbed by outside noises, gently bring your attention back to the easy, natural rhythm of your breathing. If you have trouble keeping your mind on your breath, count each inhalation and exhalation up to ten, and then start over again.

5.   As you relax physically, you may find that various feelings come and go. They shouldn't be repressed, but the very act of calmly observing them may cause them to gradually lose their intensity.

6.   Gradually intuit and then visualize a particular ahimsic quality or qualities you wish to have as the keynote of your day: patience, holding to truth, forgiveness, compassion, understanding. Express your desire to the higher self or "God within" to make this quality an integral part of your life during the day, either in silence or out loud. "I want to (or "I pray to") be sensitive to those around me and feel my compassion towards them during the day." Repeat this visualization slowly several times, and express other desires or inner yearnings which you want to integrate into your life during the day. These expressions help us to better adapt to our outer environment from a

place of inner stability and positive intent.

7.   After having expressed your keynote quality or qualities, relax and be receptive once more. Continue your relaxed, deep breathing for at least three minutes and feel this core quality or qualities as living inside your body, near the heart.

8.   This phase may be followed by repeating a sound, known in India as a *mantra*. You may choose to repeat the Sanskrit word OM three times slowly (one time per slow exhalation). This is the most sacred word in the Buddhist tradition. You can also use the word *ahimsa* or *shanti* (the Sanskrit word for peace); an English word like Peace, One, Harmony, Right Action, or a complete phrase like "Thy Will be Done." Several specialized invocations for peace can be found in Appendix 1.

9.   Visualize the feelings of peace, harmony and love streaming out into the room, the house, the neighborhood, the town or city, the region and further outward into the world. Realize that by meditating for peace, we are joining with other people around the world who are working for the same goal.

10.   Spend another minute or so in a receptive state, and end your meditation gradually and in silence.

You may want to practice this simple form of meditation for ten minutes to start, and if it feels comfortable, work up to fifteen or twenty minutes later on. For best results, try to experience this 'quiet time' with yourself at least once a day at a regular time and place. If you cannot spend ten minutes a day on contemplation or meditation, try to devote two minutes or five minutes. Meditation for peace should be a pleasure and not a chore.

In a society that places tremendous emphasis on outer accomplishments, such as fame, money and the accumulation of property, the quiet and very personal goal of gaining inner healing through ahimsa is both important and lasting.

As we work to integrate the essence of truth and compassion into our daily lives, we come closer to our natural birthright as wise and loving human beings. As brothers and sisters to all life, we become powerful agents for furthering planetary healing. Ahimsa towards oneself is for many the important first step in learning how to walk in harmony upon the Earth Mother and to help to create a peaceful world.

Peace to All Beings.

Bibliography

CHAPTER I

Albert, David H., *People Power: Applying Nonviolence Theory* (Philadelphia: New Society Publishers, 1985)

Altman, Nathaniel, *Ahimsa (Dynamic Compassion)* (Wheaton, IL: Quest Books, 1980)

Bondurant, Joan V., *Conquest of Violence* (Berkeley: University of California Press, 1971)

Carus, Paul, *Gospel of Buddha* (Tucson: Omen Communications, 1972)

Charles, Joy, ed., *Schweitzer: An Anthology* (Boston: Beacon Press, 1969)

Gandhi, M. K., *All Men Are Brothers* (Ahmedabad: Navajivan Publishing House, 1960)

Iyer, Raghavan, *The Moral and Political Thought of Mahatma Gandhi* (New York: Oxford University Press, 1973)

Jain, Champat Rai, *Fundamentals of Jainism* (Meerut: VeerNirvan Bharti, 1974)

Kotturan, George, *Ahimsa: Gautama to Gandhi* (New Delhi: Sterling, 1973)

McAllister, Pat, ed., *Reweaving the Web of Life: Feminism and Nonviolence* (Philadelphia: New Society Publishers, 1982)

Mische, Gerald and Patricia, *Toward a Human World Order* (New York: Paulist Press, 1977)

Sandu, Swaran S., Nonviolence in Indian Religious Thought and Political Action (Philadelphia: Dorrance and Co., 1977)

Tahtinen, Unto, *Ahimsa* (London: Rider and Co., 1976)

Tolstoy, Leo, *The Kingdom of God is Within You* (New York: Noonday Press, 1961)

CHAPTER 2

Bokser, Ben Zion, ed., *Abraham Isaac Kook* (New York: Paulist Press, 1978)

Chitrabhanu, Jain Master Chitrabhanu Speaks to One World (Bombay: Divine Life Society)

Gladwell, Malcolm, The Tipping Point (New York: Little Brown, 2000).

Keyes, Ken, Jr., *The Hundredth Monkey* (St Mary's: Vision Books, 1982)

Morley, S. M. and Gilliam, O. L., eds., *Respect for Life* (New York: Myrin Institute Books, 1974)

Peck, M. Scott, *People of the Lie* (New York: Simon & Schuster, 1983)

Pierrakos, Eva, *The Concept of Evil* (Phoenicia, NY: Center for the Living Force, 1965)

CHAPTER 3

Al-Ghazali, *On the Duty of Brotherhood* (Woodstock NY: Overlook Press, 1979)

Alcyone, *At the Feet of the Master* (Wheaton: Theosophical Publishing House, 1970)

Allen, Cari, *Nurse.com West*, November-December, 2016.

Bhargava, Dayanand, *Jaina Ethics* (Delhi: Motilal Barnarsidass, 1968)

Harris, Sam, *Lying* (Four Elephants Press, 2011)

Hoff, John L., "Practical Friendship", *In Context,* Summer 1985

Hoffman, Gene Knudsen, *Compassionate Listening: An Exploratory Sourcebook About Conflict Resolution* (www.newconversations.net, 2012)

Krishnamurti, J., *The First and Last Freedom* (New York: Harper & Row, 1954)

Nicholson, Shirley, *Ancient Wisdom Modem Insight* (Wheaton, IL: Theosophical Publishing House, 1985)

Peace Pilgrim, *Peace Pilgrim: Her Life and Work in Her Own Words* (Santa Fe: Ocean Tree Books, 1982)
Puruker, G. de, *Golden Precepts* (San Diego, Point Loma Publications, 1971)
Rosenberg, Marshall B., *A Model for Nonviolent Communication* (Philadelphia: New Society Publishers, 1983)
Sri Ram, N., *Thoughts for Aspirants* (Adyar: Theosophical Publishing House, 1973)
Tahtinen, op. cit. (see Ch.l refs.)
Tulku, Tarthang, *A Gesture of Balance* (Emeryville, CA: Dharma Publishing, 1977)

CHAPTER 4
Cambridge Women's Peace Collective, *My Country is the Whole World* (London and Boston: Pandora Press, 1984)
Do it Yourself Minister: Implementing a Non-Nuclear Defense Policy in a Nuclear World (Woodstock: Oxford Research Group, 1987)
Evans, Bill, About Turn: The Alternative Use of Defence Workers' Skills (London: Pluto Press, 1986)
Gowan, Suzanne *et al.*, *Moving Toward a New Society* (Philadelphia: New Society Press, 1976)
King, Martin Luther, Jr., 'Pilgrimage to Nonviolence', *The Christian Century,* 13 April 1960
Peace Pilgrim, op. cit. (see Ch. 3 refs.)
Piecing it Together: Feminism and Nonviolence (Westward Ho, Devon: Feminism and Nonviolence Study Group, 1983)
Slater, Philip, *The Pursuit of Loneliness* (Boston: Beacon Press, 1970)

CHAPTER 5

Beck, Peggy and Walters, Anna L., *The Sacred* (Tsaile, Navaho Nation, AZ: Navaho Community College Press, 1977)

Center for Science in the Public Interest, *99 Ways to a Simple Lifestyle* (Garden City: Anchor Press/Doubleday, 1977)

Gowan, Suzanne, *et al,* op. cit. (see Ch. 4 refs.)

Guatemala (New York: North American Congress on Central America, 1977)

Krishnamurti, *J., Commentaries on Living,* Volume 3 (Wheaton, IL: Quest Books, 1967)

Lappe, Frances Moore and Collins, Joseph, *Food First* (Boston: Houghton Mifflin Co., 1977 and London: Abacus Books, 1982)

Motivation and Emotion, February, 2014.

Prabhu, R. K. and Rao, U. R., eds., *The Mind of Mahatma Gandhi* (Ahmedabad: Navajivan Publishing House, 1967)

Schumacher, Fritz, *Small is Beautiful* (New York: Harper & Row, 1973 and London: Abacus Books 1974)

Slater, Philip, *Wealth Addiction* (New York: E. P. Dutton, 1980)

Trungpa, Chogyam, *Cutting through Spiritual Materialism* (Berkeley: Shambhala Publications, 1973)

Vanden Broeck, Goldian, ed., *Less is More* (New York: Harper & Row, 1978)

CHAPTER 6

Albert, David H., *People Power: Applying Nonviolent Theory* (Philadelphia: New Society Publishers, 1985)

Brock-Utne, Birgit, *Educating for Peace: A Feminist Perspective* (Elmsford, NY: Pergamon Press, 1985)

Coover, Virginia *et al., Resource Manual for a Living Revolution* (Philadelphia: New Society Publishers, 1985)

Diwaker, R. R., *Satyagraha - Its Technique and Theory* (Hinsdale IL: Henry Regnery, 1948)

Green, Duncan, *How Change Happens* (Oxford: Oxford University Press, 2016)

Joans, Lynne, ed., *Keeping the Peace* (London: Women's Press, 1983)

King, Martin Luther, Jr., *Stride Toward Peace* (New York: Harper & Row, 1958)

McAllister, Pat, op. cit. (see Ch.l refs.)

Macy, Joanna Rogers, *Despair and Personal Power in the Nuclear Age* (Philadelphia: New Society Publishers, 1983)

Peace Pilgrim, *Steps Toward Inner Peace* (Hemet, CA: Friends of Peace Pilgrim, n.d.)

Peavy, Fran *et al, Heart Politics* (Philadelphia: New Society Publishers, 1986)

Political Science Committee, *Looking In, Speaking Out* (New York: Institute of the New Age, 1978)

Remnick, David, "It Happened Here," *The New Yorker*, November 28, 2016.

Sharp, Gene, *The Politics of Nonviolent Action* [in three parts] (Boston: Porter Sargent, 1973)

Making the Abolition of War a Realistic Goal (New York: World Policy Institute,   1980)

Trungpa, Chogyam, *Shambhala: The Sacred Path of the Warrior* (Boulder: Shambhala Publications, 1984)

CHAPTER 7

Ahimsa, August 1971

Akers, Keith, *The Vegetarian Sourcebook* (New York: Putnam, 1983)

Altman, Nathaniel, *Total Vegetarian Cooking* (New Canaan, CT: Keats Publishing, 1981); *Eating for Life*

(Wheaton, IL: Quest Books, 1973 and New York: Vegetus Books, 1984)

Braunstein, Mark, *Radical Vegetarianism* (Los Angeles: Panjandrum Books, 1981)

Buchwald, Ellen Ewald, *Recipes for a Small Planet* (New York: Ballantine Books, 1973)

Giehl, Dudley, *Vegetarianism: A Way of Life* (New York: Harper & Row, 1979)

Gold, Mark, *Assault and Battery* (London: Pluto Press, 1983)

Hall, Rebecca, *Voiceless Victims* (Hounslow: Wildwood House,1984)

Harrison, Ruth, *Animal Machines* (London: Vincent Stuart, 1964)

Mason, Jim, and Singer, Peter, *Animal Factories* (New York: Crown Publishers, 1982)

Moran, Victoria, *Compassion: The Ultimate Ethic* (Wellingborough: Thorsons, 1985)

Robertson, Laurel *et al., Laurel's Kitchen* (New York: Bantam Books, 1978)

Rosen, Steven, *Food for the Spirit* (New York: Bala Books, 1987)

Singer, Peter, *Animal Liberation* (New York: Avon Books, 1977)

Vegetarian Diets (Washington: National Research Council, 1974)

Wynne-Tyson, John, *Food for a Future* (London: Sphere, 1976)

CHAPTER 8

The Animals' Agenda, various issues

Arundale, George, *You* (Wheaton, IL: Quest Books, 1973)

Pratt, Dallas, *Painful Experiments on Animals* (New York: Argus Archives, 1976)

Regan, Tom, *The Case for Animal Rights* (Berkeley: University of California Press, 1984)

Ruesch, Hans, *Slaughter of the Innocent* (New York: Bantam Books, 1978)

Ryder, Richard, *Victims of Science* (London: Davis-Poyntner, 1984)

Singer, Peter, ed., *In Defense of Animals* (London and New York: Basil Blackwell, 1985)

CHAPTER 9

Amory, Cleveland, *Man Kind?* (New York: Harper & Row, 1974)

Baker, Ron, *The American Hunting Myth* (New York: Vantage, 1985)

Padover, Saul K., *Aggression Without Weapons* (New York: Ethical Culture Publications, 1968)

Regan, Tom and Singer, Peter, eds., *Animal Rights and Human Obligations* (Englewood Cliffs: Prentice-Hall, 1976)

CHAPTER 10

Animalia, July-September 1975

Beston, Henry, *The Outermost House* (New York: Holt, Rine- hardt & Winston, 1977)

Cousteau, Jacques-Yves and Dore, Philippe, *The Whale: Mighty Monarch of the Sea* (Garden City: Doubleday, 1972)

McKenna, Virgina, *et al., Beyond the Bars: The Zoo Dilemma* (Wellingborough: Thorsons, 1987)

Morell, Virginia, "Do Zoos Shorten Elephant Life Spans?" *Science*, December 11, 2008.

Robbins, Tom, *Another Roadside Attraction* (New York: Ballantine Books, 1975)

CHAPTER 11

Baker, Richard St Barbe, *Sahara Conquest* (London: Lutterworth Press, 1966)

Barker, Michael, ed., *The Directory of the Environment* (London: Routledge & Kegan Paul, 1986)

Bisch, Robert, *The Ecological Conscience* (Englewood Cliffs: Prentice-Hall, 1970)

Brown, Lester *et ah, State of the World* (New York: W. W. Norton, 1987)

Bunyard, Peter and Morgan-Grenville, Fern, *The Green Alternative Guide to Good Living* (London: Methuen, 1987)

Darling, G. and D., eds., *Stevenson* (Chicago: Contemporary Books, 1977)

D.I.Y. Conservation (Wallingford: British Trust for Conservation Volunteers, 1984)

Myers, Norman, *The Gaia Atlas of Planetary Management* (London: Pan Books, 1985)

Naimy, Mikhail, *The Book of Mirdad* (Baltimore: Penguin Books, 1971)

Porritt, Jonathon, *Seeing Green* (London: Basil Blackwell, 1985)

Friends of the Earth Handbook (London: Macdonald, 1987)

Russell, Peter, *The Global Brain* (Los Angeles: J. P. Tarcher, 1983)

Seymour, John and Girardet, Herbert, *Blueprint for a Green Planet* (London: Dorling Kindersley, 1987)

Snyder, T. P., ed., *The Biosphere Catalog* (London and Fort Worth: Synergetic Press, 1985)

CHAPTER 12

American Scientist, February 1976

Berger, John J., *Nuclear Power: The Unviable Option* (New York: Dell Publishing Co., 1977)

Brown, Lester *et al., State of the World 1984* (New York: W. W. Norton & Co., 1984)

Bunyard, Peter, op. cit. (see Ch. 11 refs.)

Caldicott, Helen, *Nuclear Madness* (New York: Bantam Books, 1980)

Center for Science in the Public Interest, op. cit. (see Ch. 5 refs.)

Coover, Virginia, *et al.,* op. cit.

Jeffs, Martin, *Manual for Action* (London: Action Resources Group, 1982)

Laszlo, Ervin *et al., Goals for Mankind* (New York: E. P. Dutton, 1977)

Lilienthal, David E., *Atomic Energy* (New York: Harper & Row, 1980)

Novick, Sheldon, *The Careless Atom* (Boston: Houghton Mifflin Co., 1969)

Patterson, Walt, *Nuclear Power* (London: Penguin Books, 1976)

Porritt, Jonathon, *Seeing Green* (London: Basil Blackwell, 1985)

Pringle, Peter, and Spigelman, James, *The Nuclear Barons* (London: Sphere Books, 1983)

Shelley, D., and Jeffries, P., *A Legal Advice Pack for Nuclear Disarmers* (London: CND, 1984)

Webb, Richard, *The Accidental Hazards of Nuclear Power Plants* (Amherst: University of Massachusetts Press, 1976)

CHAPTER 13

Besant, Annie and Leadbeater, C. W., *The Noble Eightfold Path* (Adyar: Theosophical Publishing House, 1955)

Fox, Matthew, *Compassion* (Minneapolis: Winston Press, 1979)

Goddard, Dwight, *The Buddha's Golden Path* (Albuquerque: Sun Books, 1981)

The New York Times Magazine, 11 January 1981
Perry, Danaan and Forest, Lila, *The Earthsteward's Handbook* (Monte Rio, CA: Holyearth Foundation)

CHAPTER 14

Altman, Nathaniel, *The Deva Handbook: How to Work with Nature's Subtle Energies* (Rochester VT: Destiny Books, 1995)
Benson, Herbert, *The Relaxation Response* (New York: Avon
Cousins, Norman, *Anatomy of an Illness* (New York: W. W. Norton, 1980)
Jampolsky, Gerald, *Love is Letting Go of Fear* (New York: Bantam Books, 1981)
Judge, William Q., *The Heart Doctrine* (Bombay: Theosophy Company, 1963)
Schweitzer, Albert, *Reverence for Life* (New York: Harper & Row, 1966)
Selye, Hans, *Stress Without Distress* (New York: Signet Books, 1975)
Simonton, O. Carl *et al.*, *Getting Well Again* (New York: Bantam Books, 1980)
Smoley, Richard, "Why Forgive?" *Quest* 97. 3 (Summer 2009): 102-106.
Vasto, Lanzo del, *Make Straight the Way of the Lord* (New York: Alfred A. Knopf, 1974)

Appendix 1.

Affirmations and Prayers for Peace

Pope Francis' Peace Message

Active nonviolence is a way of showing that unity is truly more powerful and more fruitful than conflict. Everything in the world is interconnected. Certainly differences can cause frictions. But let us face them constructively and nonviolently, so that tensions and oppositions can achieve a diversified and life-giving unity, preserving what is valid and useful on both sides...

-From the *Message for the Celebration of the Fiftieth Day of Peace*, 2016.

Lover of All Nations

O God of many names, lover of all nations,
We pray for peace
In our hearts, In our homes
In our nations, In our world
The peace of Your Will, The peace of our need.

To the Masters of Wisdom

O Masters of the Wisdom May Your blessing rest on us,
Your peace shine through us to all humankind.
May Your peace and blessing pour out to all in authority
that they may be wise and illumined.
May the power from this meditation flow to the World
Mind, to uplift humanity and set it onwards towards the
Light.

O Hidden Life

O Hidden Life Vibrant in Every Atom O Hidden Light,
Shining in Every Creature O Hidden Love, Embracing All
in Oneness,
May each of us who feels as One with Thee
Know that we are therefore One with every other. Amen

To the Powers of Love

O, Powers of Love, we pledge to you our faithfulness,
knowing that only Love can redeem the world.
We invoke Your blessing upon all who strive to serve you.
We invoke Your blessing upon all, who in these days of
war, have to endure suffering, and that they may joyfully
discover their enfoldment in Your love, even in the midst of
their affliction.
We invoke Your blessing upon all who willfully inflict
suffering, that they may be moved to return to you and
serve you.
O Powers of Love, we pledge to you our faithfulness.

A World Wide Blessing

1. Love to All Beings
     North - South - East - West - Above - Below
     Love to All Beings - silence -
2. Compassion to All Beings
     North - South - East - West - Above- Below
     Compassion to All Beings - silence -
3. Joy to All Beings
     North - South - East - West - Above - Below
     Joy to All Beings - silence -
4. Serenity to All Beings
     North - South - East - West - Above- Below
     Serenity to All Beings - silence -

The Great Invocation

From the point of Light within the mind of God Let Light
stream forth into the minds of all Let Light descend on
Earth
From the point of Love within the heart of God Let Love
stream forth into the hearts of all May Christ return to
Earth.
From the centre where the Will of God is known
Let purpose guide the little wills of all -
The purpose which the Masters know and serve.
From the centre which we call the race of humans Let the
Plan of Love and Light work out And may it seal the door
where evil dwells.
Let Love and Light Power Restore the Plan on Earth.

Unification Blessing

The sons and daughters of the Earth Mother are one and I
am one with them.
I seek to love, not hate;
I seek to serve and not exact due service;
I seek to heal, not hurt.
Let pain bring due reward of light and love.
Let the soul control the outer form And life and all events,
And bring to light the love
Which underlies the happenings of the time.
Let vision and insight come.
Let the future stand revealed.
Let inner union demonstrate and outer cleavages be gone.
Let love prevail.
Let all love.

Invocation for Peace

With our thoughts we make our world.
Our mind is central and precedes our deeds.

273

Speak or act with a pure mind.
And happiness will follow you
Like a shadow that never leaves.

May there be joy in the world
With bountiful harvests and spiritual wealth.
May every good fortune come to be.
And may all our wishes be fulfilled.

As long as space remains
And as long as sentient beings remain
Until then, may I, too, remain
And help dispel the misery of the world.

-His Holiness the 14th *Dalai Lama*, Tenzin Gyatso

Prayers for Peace

The following are peace prayers on behalf of some of the world's major religions, as well as indigenous peace prayers from Africa and North America. They may be used for both individual prayer and group work.

Universal Prayer for Peace

Lead me from Death to Life
From Falsehood to Truth
Lead me from despair to Hope
from Fear to trust
Lead me from Hate to Love
from war to Peace
Let Peace fill our Heart,
our World, our Universe.
Amen.

Baha'i Prayer for Peace

Be generous in prosperity,
and thankful in adversity.
Be fair in judgment,
and guarded in thy speech,
Be a lamp unto those who walk
in darkness, and a home
to the stranger.
Be eyes to the blind, and a guiding light
unto the feet of the erring
Be a breath of life to the body of
humankind, a dew to the soil of
the human heart,
and a fruit upon the tree of humility.

Buddhist Prayer for Peace

May all beings everywhere plagued with sufferings of body and mind
quickly be freed from their illnesses.
May those frightened cease to be afraid, and may those bound be free.
May the powerless find power, and may people think of befriending one another.
May those who find themselves in trackless, fearful wilderness- the children, the aged, the unprotected-- be guarded by beneficial celestials, and may they swiftly attain Buddhahood.

Catholic Prayer for Peace

Lord, make me an instrument of Your peace.
Where there is hatred, let me sow love;
where there is injury, pardon;
where there is doubt, faith;

where there is despair, hope;
where there is darkness, light;
where there is sadness, joy.

O, Divine Master, grant that I may not so much seek to be consoled as to console; to be understood as to understand; to be loved as to love; For it is in giving that we receive; it is in pardoning that we are pardoned; it is in dying that we are born again to eternal life.

Christian Prayer for Peace

Blessed are the peacemakers, for they shall be known as the Children of God.
But I say to you that hear, love your enemies, do good to those who hate you,
bless those who curse you;
pray for those who abuse you;
To those that strike you on the cheek, offer the other one also,
and from those who take away your cloak, do not withhold your coat as well.
Give to everyone who begs from you, and of those who take away your goods,
do not ask for them again.
And as you wish that others would do to you, do so to them.

Indigenous African Prayer for Peace

Almighty God, the Great Thumb we cannot evade to tie any knot;
The Roaring Thunder that splits mighty trees:
The all-seeing Lord up on high who sees even the footprints of an antelope on
a rock mass here on Earth.

You are the one who does not hesitate to respond to our call.
You are the cornerstone of peace.

Hindu Prayer for Peace

Oh God, lead us from the unreal to the Real.
Oh God, lead us from darkness to light.
Oh God, lead us from death to immortality.
Shanti, Shanti, Shanti unto all.
Oh Lord God almighty, may there be peace in celestial regions.
May there be peace on Earth.
May the waters be appeasing.
May herbs be wholesome, and may trees and other plants bring peace to all.
May all beneficent beings bring peace to us.
May thy Vedic Law propagate peace all through the world.
May all things be a source of peace to us.
And may thy peace itself, bestow peace on all, and may that peace come to me also.

Jain Prayer for Peace

Peace and Universal Love is the essence of the Gospel preached by all Enlightened Ones.
The Lord has preached that equanimity is the Dharma.
Forgive do I creatures all, and let all creatures forgive me.
Unto all have I amity, and unto none enmity.
Know that violence is the root cause of all the misery in the world.
Violence, in fact, is the knot of bondage.
"Do not injure any living being."
This is the eternal, perennial, and unalterable way of spiritual life.
A weapon, howsoever powerful it may be,

can always be superseded by a superior one;
but no weapon can, however,
be superior to non-violence and love.

Jewish Prayer for Peace

Come, let us go up to the mountain of the Lord, that we may walk the paths of the Most High.
And we shall beat our swords into ploughshares, and our spears into pruning hooks.
Nation shall not lift up sword against nation-
neither shall they learn war any more.
And none shall be afraid, for the mouth of the Lord of Hosts has spoken.

Muslim Prayer for Peace

In the name of Allah, the beneficent, the merciful.
Praise be to the Lord of the Universe who has created us and
made us into tribes and nations;
That we may know each other, not that we may despise each other.
If the enemy inclines towards peace, do thou also incline towards peace, and trust God, for the Lord is the one that hears and knows all things.
And the servants of God, Most gracious are those who walk on the Earth in humility, and when we address them, we say "peace."

Native American Prayer for Peace

O Great Spirit of our Ancestors,
I raise my pipe to you.
To your messengers the four winds, and to Mother Earth who provides for your children.

Give us the wisdom to teach our children to love, to respect, and to be kind to each other so that they may grow with peace of mind.
Let us learn to share all good things that you provide for us on this Earth.

Shintō Prayer for Peace

Although the people living across the ocean surrounding us,
I believe, are all our brothers and sisters.
Why are there constant troubles in this world?
Why do winds and waves rise in the oceans surrounding us?
I only earnestly wish that the wind will soon whisk away all the clouds
which are hanging over the tops of the mountains.

Sikh Prayer for Peace

God adjudges us according to our deeds,
not the coat that we wear:
that Truth is above everything,
but higher still is truthful living.
Know that we attain God when we love,
and only victory endures in consequences of which no one is defeated.

Zoroastrian Prayer for Peace

We pray to God to eradicate all the misery in the world;
that understanding triumph over ignorance,
that generosity triumph over indifference,
that trust triumph over contempt, and
that truth triumph over falsehood.

Adapted from the Fellowship of Faith's Prayer for Peace

May Peace and Prosperity return among us,
May Cooperation unite us, love bind us,
Brotherhood enfold us, Patience possess us,
Self-control strengthen us, the Past be forgiven us,
The Future be sanctified for us,
May Peace and prosperity return to us!

The Work of Peace

Give us courage, O Lord, to stand up and be counted,
to stand up for those who cannot stand up for themselves,
to stand up for ourselves when it is needful for us to do so.
Let us fear nothing more than we fear you.
Let us love nothing more than we love you,
for thus we shall fear nothing also.
Let us have no other God before you.
Whether nation or party of state or church.
Let us seek no other peace but the peace which is yours,
and make us its instruments,
opening our eyes and our ears and our hearts,
so that we should know always what work of peace we may
do for you.

-By Alan Paton, author of *Cry the Beloved Country*, a powerful
novel about apartheid in South Africa.

Peace Pilgrim's Ways of Prayer

You can visualize God's light each day and send it to
someone who needs help. Your divine nature must reach
out and touch the divine nature of another. Within you is
the light of the world, it must be shared with the world.

Visualize a golden light within you and spread it out. First to those around you- your circle of friends and relatives- and then gradually to the world. Keep on visualizing God's golden light surrounding our earth.

And if you have a problem, take the matter to God in prayer, and visualize it in God's hands. Then leave it, knowing it is in the best possible hands, and turn your attention to other things.

-From *Peace Pilgrim: Her Life and Work in Her Own Words* (Ocean Tree Books, 1991)

Peace Pilgrim

Appendix 2: Organizations and Publications

The following listing contains the names and web sites of a number of organizations and publications that are in harmony with the ideas set forth in this book. I have organized them according to location, although physical location does not necessarily define the scope of their work. If any organizations have been inadvertently left out, please let me know, and they will be considered for listing in future editions.

UNITED STATES

American Anti-Vivisection Society, publishes *AV*.
www.aavc.org
American Friends Service Committee (Quakers).
www.afsc.org
American Vegan Society, publishes *Ahimsa*.
www.americanvegan.org
Amnesty International USA. www.amnestyusa.org/
Animals' Agenda. www.animalsagenda.org/
Beauty Without Cruelty. www.beautywithoutcruelty.com/
Born Free USA. www.bornfreeusa.org/
The Catholic Worker Movement, publishes *The Catholic Worker*. *www.catholicworker.org*
Center for Study of Responsive Law. http://csrl.org/
Committee to Abolish Sport Hunting. www.all-creatures.org/cash/
Compassion in World Farming. www.ciwf.com/
The Compassionate Listening Project.
www.compassionatelistening.org/
Earthstewards Network. www.earthstewards.org/
Environmental Action. http://environmental-action.org/
Essential Partners. www.publicconversations.org/

Farm Animal Rights Movement. www.farmusa.org/
Fellowship for Reconciliation. www.forusa.org/
Food First [Institute for Food and Development Policy].
https://foodfirst.org/
Friends of the Earth. www.foe.org/
Fund for Animals. www.fundforanimals.org/
Greenpeace. www.greenpeace.org/usa/
Green America. www.greenamerica.org/
In Defense of Animals. www.idausa.org/
Institute for Defense and Disarmament Studies.
www.idds.org/
International Society for Animal Rights.
http://isaronline.org/
Karuna Center for Peacebuilding. www.karunacenter.org/
King Center for Nonviolent Social Change.
www.thekingcenter.org/
National Anti-Vivisection Society. www.navs.org/
The National Coalition for Dialogue & Deliberation.
http://ncdd.org/
National War Tax Resistance Coordination Committee.
http://nwtrcc.org/
Nonviolence International.
http://nonviolenceinternational.net/
Nonviolent Communication / Puddle Dancer Press.
www.nonviolentcommunication.com/index.htm
North American Vegetarian Society, publishes *Vegetarian Voice*. https://navs-online.org/
Nuclear Age Peace Foundation. www.wagingpeace.org/
Oxfam America. www.oxfamamerica.org/
Peace Development Fund.
www.peacedevelopmentfund.org/
People for the Ethical Treatment of Animals (PETA).
www.peta.org/
Physicians for Social Responsibility. www.psr.org/
Planetary Citizens. www.planetarycitizens.org/home.html
Praxis Peace Institute. www.praxispeace.org/

Sea Shepherd Conservation Society.
www.seashepherd.org/
Sierra Club. www.sierraclub.org/
Sojourners. https://sojo.net/
Soulforce. www.soulforce.org/
Theosophical Order of Service. www.theoservice.org/
Tikkun, publishes *Tikkun*. www.tikkun.org/
Union of Concerned Scientists. www.ucsusa.org/
Vegetarian Resource Group, publishes *Vegetarian Journal*.
www.vrg.org/
War Resisters' League. www.warresisters.org/
Women's International League for Peace and Freedom.
http://wilpf.org/
World Goodwill / Lucis Trust.
www.lucistrust.org/world_goodwill
Worldwatch Institute. www.worldwatch.org/
Yes! Magazine. www.yesmagazine.org/

AUSTRALIA

Animal Liberation. www.animal-lib.org.au/
Animals Australia. http://animalsaustralia.org/
Australia Vegetarian Society. www.veg-soc.org.au/
Choose Cruelty Free. www.choosecrueltyfree.org.au/
Friends of the Earth. www.foe.org.au/
Greenpeace Australia Pacific.
www.greenpeace.org/australia/en/
Men of the Trees. www.menofthetrees.com.au/
People for Nuclear Disarmament. www.pndnsw.org.au/
Social Alternatives (publication).
http://socialalternatives.com/home
The Vegan Society in Australia. www.veganaustralia.net/
Women's International League for Peace and Freedom.
www.wilpf.org.au/

CANADA

Amnesty International. www.amnesty.ca/
Animal Defense League of Canada. http://animal-defence.ncf.ca/
Ark II - Canadian Animal Rights Network. www.ark-ii.com/index.php/en/
Canadian Peace Congress. www.canadianpeacecongress.ca/
Friends of the Earth. http://foecanada.org/en/
Green Party of Canada. www.greenparty.ca/
Greenpeace Foundation. www.greenpeace.org/canada/en/home/
Peace and Environment Resource Centre. www.perc.ca/
Peace Magazine (publication). www.peacemagazine.org/
Project Ploughshares. http://ploughshares.ca/
Science for Peace. http://scienceforpeace.ca/

INDIA

Ekta Parishad. http://ektaparishad.com/
Nelson Mandela Centre for Peace and Conflict Resolution. http://jmi.ac.in/cpcr

NEW ZEALAND

Conservation Volunteers New Zealand. http://conservationvolunteers.co.nz/
Friends of the Earth. www.foei.org/member-groups/asia-pacific/new-zealand
Go Vegan. http://govegan.org.nz/
New Zealand Ecological Society. http://newzealandecology.org/
The Peace Foundation. www.peace.net.nz/

New Zealand Vegetarian Society. www.vegetarian.org.nz/
SAFE for Animals. http://safe.org.nz/
Royal New Zealand SPCA. www.rnzspca.org.nz/
Wellington Campaign for Nuclear Disarmament.
    www.converge.org.nz/pma/cnd/
Women's International League for Peace and Freedom.
    www.converge.org.nz/pma/wilpf/

UNITED KINGDOM

Amnesty International. www.amnesty.org.uk/
Animal Aid. www.animalaid.org.uk/h/n/AA/HOME/
Animal Liberation Front (ALF).
www.animalliberationfront.com/
Beauty Without Cruelty. www.bwcshop.com/
Campaign for Nuclear Disarmament (CND).
www.cnduk.org/
Compassion in World Farming. www.ciwf.org.uk/
Conscience (peace tax campaign).
www.conscienceonline.org.uk/
The Conservation Volunteers. www.tcv.org.uk/
Cruelty Free International.
www.crueltyfreeinternational.org/
The Ecologist (publication). www.theecologist.org/
European Group for Ecological Action (Ecorpora).
www.ecoropa.info/
Findhorn Foundation. www.findhorn.org/
Friends of the Earth. www.foe.co.uk/
Green Alliance. www.green-alliance.org.uk/
Greenpeace. www.green-alliance.org.uk/
Hunt Saboteurs' Association. www.huntsabs.org.uk/
International Vegetarian Union (IVU). www.ivu.org/
Jewish Vegetarian Society. www.jvs.org.uk/
National Anti-Vivisection Society Ltd.
www.navs.org.uk/home/
Oxfam. www.oxfam.org.uk/

Houseman's Peace Diary (publication).
www.housmans.com/diary.php
Peace News (publication). http://peacenews.info/
Peace Pledge Union. www.ppu.org.uk/
Resurgence & Ecologist (publication).
www.resurgence.org/
The Vegan Society. www.vegansociety.com/
 The Vegetarian Society of the UK Ltd. www.vegsoc.org/
War Resisters International. www.wri-irg.org/

"INTERNATIONAL"

Alternatives to Violence International.
http://avp.international/
Center for Applied Nonviolent Action and Strategies.
http://canvasopedia.org/
Center for Nonviolent Communication. www.cnvc.org/
Center for Partnership Studies.
http://centerforpartnership.org/
Conscience and Peace Tax International (CPTI).
www.cpti.ws/
Nonviolence Peaceforce, Protecting civilians in violent
conflicts through unarmed strategies.
www.nonviolentpeaceforce.org/
Nonviolence Project. http://nonviolence.com/
Pax Christi International. www.paxchristi.net/
Peace Brigades International. www.peacebrigades.org/
Peace Revolution. https://peacerevolution.net/
Theosophical Order of Service International.
www.international.theoservice.org/
Transcend International: A Peace Development
Environment Network.
Transforming Violence. www.transformingviolence.org/

About the Author

NATHANIEL ALTMAN is a Brooklyn, New York -based writer, teacher and counselor who has authored more than twenty books on peace studies, healthy diets, alternative healing, nature and relationship. His books include *Eating for Life* (Quest Books, 1973, 1977; Vegetus 1984), *Ahimsa: Dynamic Compassion* (Quest, 1980), *Sacred Trees* (Sierra Club Books, 1994, Sterling Publishing, 1999), *The Twelve Stages of Healing* [with Donald M. Epstein, D.C.] (New World Library, 1994), *The Deva Handbook* (Destiny Books, 1995), *The Little Giant Encyclopedia of Meditations and Blessings* (Sterling Publishing, 2000), *Healing Springs* (Healing Arts, 2000), *Sacred Water* (HiddenSpring, 2002), *The Honey Prescription* (Healing Arts, 2010) and *The New Oxygen Prescription* (Healing Arts, 2017).

A student of political science and metaphysics for over 40 years, Nathaniel is a writer, lecturer and workshop leader. He was a faculty member at the Krotona School of Theosophy in Ojai, California, and has appeared on over 150 radio and television programs throughout the United States and Canada, Australia, Latin America and Europe. His articles have appeared in a variety of publications, including *Good Housekeeping, Natural Health, Well Being, Free Spirit, Vegetarian Times* and *USA Today*.

Nathaniel's website is www.nathanielaltman.com

CPSIA information can be obtained
at www.ICGtesting.com
Printed in the USA
FSHW022225050520
69959FS